Everyday Simple Air Fryer Cookbook for Beginners

Quick, Low-Calorie, Dump-and-Go Recipes with a 28-Day Meal Plan — Fry, Roast, and Bake with Ingredients from Your Cupboard for One, Two, or Family Meals

Contents

Copyright Disclaimer

Copyright © 2024 by Lisa Larsen. All rights reserved.

Introduction

Welcome to the **Everyday Simple Air Fryer Cookbook for Beginners!** This cookbook is crafted specifically for those who are new to air frying or for anyone seeking to create easy, healthy, and delicious meals that fit into their busy lifestyles. If you're looking for a way to enjoy flavorful meals without the hassle of complicated recipes or hard-to-find ingredients, you've arrived at the right place!

The Air Fryer Revolution

The air fryer has quickly become a staple in modern kitchens, and for good reason. This innovative appliance allows you to fry, roast, bake, and grill food using hot air circulation, producing crispy and flavorful dishes without the excess oil. Imagine indulging in your favorite fried foods while significantly cutting down on fat and calories! This means you can savor the taste you love without the guilt.

What's Inside?

In this cookbook, you'll find an extensive collection of over 200 fast and easy recipes that are ideal for families and individuals. Whether you're cooking for yourself, for two, or for a larger family, these recipes are designed to be simple, nutritious, and satisfying.

Key Features:
- **Fast and Easy Daily Favorites:** Quick meals that are perfect for any day of the week, with a variety of options that cater to different tastes.

- **DumpandGo Recipes:** These recipes require minimal prep time—simply throw the ingredients into the air fryer and let it work its magic!

- **Basic Ingredients:** All recipes utilize common pantry staples, making them affordable and convenient.

- **LowCalorie and LowFat Options:** Healthconscious meals that don't compromise on flavor.

- **Versatile Cooking Methods:** Learn how to fry, roast, and bake, expanding your cooking repertoire.

Why Air Frying?

Cooking with an air fryer is not just about convenience; it's about enhancing your culinary experience. This book will guide you through each recipe, providing stepbystep instructions and helpful tips to ensure your success in the kitchen.

What is an Air Fryer and How Does It Work?

An air fryer is a countertop kitchen appliance that mimics the results of deep frying using hot air. At its core, it consists of a heating element and a powerful fan that circulates hot air around the food, creating a crispy exterior while keeping the inside moist and tender.

How It Works:

- **Convection Heating:** The air fryer uses convection heat to cook food. The heating element heats the air inside the fryer, and the fan circulates this hot air around the food at high speeds. This results in an even cooking temperature and helps to achieve that desirable crispy texture.

- **Oil Usage:** Unlike traditional frying, which requires submerging food in hot oil, air frying only needs a small amount of oil or even none at all. You can lightly coat your food with oil or use cooking spray for added flavor without the added calories. Some recipes may not require any oil, making them lighter and healthier.

Setting Up Your New Air Fryer

Setting up your air fryer is simple and straightforward. Follow these steps to get started:

1. **Unpack and Inspect:** Carefully remove your air fryer from its packaging. Inspect it for any visible damage or missing parts. Ensure you have all the components, including the basket, tray, and any additional accessories.

2. **Choose a Suitable Location:** Place the air fryer on a flat, stable surface in your kitchen, away from any heat sources or flammable materials. Ensure there is adequate space around the appliance for air circulation.

3. **Read the Manual:** Before using your air fryer for the first time, take a few minutes to read the user manual. This will familiarize you with its features, settings, and safety precautions.

4. **Clean Before Use:** Wash the cooking basket and tray with warm, soapy water to remove any dust or residues from manufacturing. Rinse and dry them thoroughly before using.

5. **Initial Test Run:** To eliminate any manufacturing odors, run the air fryer at a high temperature (around 400°F or 200°C) for about 15 minutes without any food. This helps to preheat the appliance and ensure it's ready for cooking.

How Air Fryers Differ and Cooking Options

Air fryers come in various models and styles, each with its unique features and functionalities. Here are some common differences:

- **Size and Capacity:** Air fryers vary in size, ranging from compact models suitable for one or two people to larger ones that can cook for families. Consider your cooking needs when choosing a size.

- **Cooking Technology:** While most air fryers use convection heat, some models feature advanced technology, such as digital controls, multiple cooking presets, and additional functions like rotisserie or dehydrating.

- **Design Features:** Air fryers come in different designs, including basket-style and oven-style. Basket-style air fryers are more common and easy to use, while oven-style models often provide more cooking space and versatility.

Cooking Methods with an Air Fryer

Air fryers are versatile appliances that allow for various cooking methods:

1. **Frying:** Air fryers excel at creating crispy fried foods with little to no oil. You can fry items like chicken wings, french fries, and onion rings with delicious results.

2. **Roasting:** You can roast vegetables, meats, and poultry, achieving that caramelized exterior and tender interior without the need for a traditional oven. Roasted Brussels sprouts or a whole chicken can be easily prepared in an air fryer.

3. **Baking:** Many air fryers can bake cookies, muffins, and cakes, making them a great alternative to conventional ovens. The hot air circulation helps create an even bake, resulting in delightful baked goods.

4. **Grilling:** Some air fryers come with grill plates or grates, allowing you to achieve a grilled effect on meats and vegetables. You can make grilled kebabs or burgers in no time.

5. **Reheating:** Use your air fryer to reheat leftovers quickly and efficiently. The air fryer restores crispiness that microwaves often leave soggy.

Advantages and Disadvantages of an Air Fryer

Advantages:

- **Healthier Cooking:** Air frying drastically reduces the amount of oil needed, leading to lower calorie meals that are less greasy. This can help you meet your health goals without sacrificing flavor.

- **Versatility:** The air fryer isn't just for frying; it can roast vegetables, bake cookies, and even reheat leftovers. This multi-functionality makes it a valuable tool in your kitchen.

- **Quick Cooking Time:** Air fryers generally cook food faster than traditional ovens due to their efficient heat circulation. This is particularly beneficial for busy families or individuals.

- **Ease of Use:** Most air fryers come equipped with user-friendly controls and preset cooking options, making them accessible for beginners. The simple interface allows you to set time and temperature with minimal effort.

Disadvantages:

- **Capacity Limitations:** Air fryers typically have a smaller cooking capacity compared to conventional ovens, which may require you to cook in batches if you're preparing meals for larger families or gatherings.

- **Texture Differences:** While air-fried foods can be crispy, they may not achieve the exact texture of deep-fried foods, particularly when it comes to battered items. It may take some experimentation to find the perfect methods and recipes that suit your taste.

- **Learning Curve:** If you're used to traditional cooking methods, it may take time to adapt recipes for the air fryer. Understanding cooking times and temperatures is essential for successful results.

Health Benefits of Air Frying

Using an air fryer can offer numerous health benefits:

- **Lower Fat Content:** The reduced need for oil in air frying translates to fewer calories, making it easier to enjoy traditionally high-calorie foods without the guilt.

- **Nutrient Retention:** Air frying often requires shorter cooking times, which helps to preserve the vitamins and minerals in fruits and vegetables. This means you can enjoy meals that are both flavorful and nutritious.

- **Satisfying Meals:** You can indulge in a wide variety of dishes—from crispy vegetables to tender meats—without compromising your health goals.

What Cannot Be Cooked in an Air Fryer?

While air fryers are incredibly versatile, there are certain foods that are not ideal for cooking in them:

- **Battered Foods:** Foods with a wet batter, like tempura or certain types of fried chicken, may not cook well and can create a mess inside the air fryer.

- **Leafy Greens:** Delicate items like spinach or lettuce can easily blow around in the circulating air, resulting in uneven cooking and a burnt taste.

- **Cheese:** While you can use cheese in dishes, whole pieces of cheese may melt and create a mess. Instead, incorporate cheese into recipes where it can be contained, such as stuffed items.

How to Clean and Maintain Your Air Fryer

Proper maintenance is essential for your air fryer to function optimally and last for years to come. Here's how to clean and maintain it effectively:

- **Unplug and Cool Down:** Always unplug the air fryer and allow it to cool completely before cleaning to avoid burns.

- **Remove and Wash Accessories:** Take out the cooking basket and tray. Wash them in warm, soapy water or place them in the dishwasher (if dishwasher-safe) for easy cleaning.

- **Wipe the Exterior:** Use a damp cloth to wipe down the outside of the air fryer. Avoid abrasive cleaners or scrubbers that could scratch the surface.

- **Deep Cleaning:** For stubborn residues, soak the basket and tray in warm soapy water for about 15-20 minutes, then scrub with a soft sponge to remove any stuck-on food. For the heating element, gently wipe it with a damp cloth; ensure no moisture gets inside the appliance.

- **Check for Wear and Tear:** Regularly inspect the power cord and plug for any damage. If you notice any issues, discontinue use and consult the manufacturer's guidelines.

By following these cleaning and maintenance tips, you can ensure your air fryer remains in excellent condition, ready to create delicious meals for you and your family.

Chapter 2

Breakfast Favourites

1. Breakfast Potatoes

 Yield:
4 servings

 Prep time:
10 minutes

 Cook time:
20 minutes

 Cooking Temperature:
400°F (200°C)

Cooking Method:
Roast

Ingredients:

- 2 cups diced potatoes
- 1 tablespoon olive oil
- 1 teaspoon garlic powder
- 1 teaspoon paprika
- Salt and pepper to taste

Nutritional Information

130 calories, 3g protein, 23g carbohydrates, 3g fat, 2g fiber, 0mg cholesterol, 230mg sodium, 450mg potassium.

Directions:

1. Preheat the air fryer to 400°F (200°C).
2. In a bowl, toss diced potatoes with olive oil, garlic powder, paprika, salt, and pepper.
3. Place the potatoes in the air fryer basket in a single layer.
4. Cook for 20 minutes, shaking the basket halfway through.

2. Egg Muffins

 Yield:
4 servings

 Prep time:
10 minutes

 Cook time:
15 minutes

 Cooking Temperature:
350°F (175°C)

Cooking Method:
Bake

Ingredients:

- 6 large eggs
- 1/2 cup diced bell peppers
- 1/4 cup diced onion
- 1/2 cup spinach, chopped
- Salt and pepper to taste

Nutritional Information

80 calories, 6g protein, 2g carbohydrates, 5g fat, 1g fiber, 186mg cholesterol, 160mg sodium, 150mg potassium.

Directions:

1. Preheat the air fryer to 350°F (175°C).
2. In a bowl, whisk together eggs, bell peppers, onion, spinach, salt, and pepper.
3. Pour the mixture into silicone muffin cups.
4. Place the cups in the air fryer and cook for 15 minutes.

3. Oatmeal Cups

 Yield:
4 servings

 Prep time:
5 minutes

 Cook time:
15 minutes

 Cooking Temperature:
350°F (175°C)

 Cooking Method:
Bake

Ingredients:

- 2 cups rolled oats
- 2 cups almond milk (or regular milk)
- 1/2 teaspoon cinnamon
- 1/4 cup honey or maple syrup
- 1/2 cup mixed berries

Nutritional Information

150 calories, 5g protein, 27g carbohydrates, 3g fat, 4g fiber, 0mg cholesterol, 70mg sodium, 200mg potassium.

Directions:

1. Preheat the air fryer to 350°F (175°C).
2. In a bowl, mix rolled oats, milk, cinnamon, and honey/maple syrup.
3. Spoon the mixture into silicone muffin cups and top with berries.
4. Cook in the air fryer for 15 minutes.

4. Banana Bread

 Yield:
6 servings

 Prep time:
10 minutes

 Cook time:
30 minutes

 Cooking Temperature:
320°F (160°C)

 Cooking Method:
Bake

Ingredients:

- 2 ripe bananas, mashed
- 1/2 cup applesauce
- 1/2 cup flour (whole wheat or all-purpose)
- 1/2 teaspoon baking soda
- 1/4 teaspoon salt

Nutritional Information

140 calories, 2g protein, 28g carbohydrates, 1g fat, 2g fiber, 0mg cholesterol, 150mg sodium, 200mg potassium.

Directions:

1. Preheat the air fryer to 320°F (160°C).
2. In a bowl, combine mashed bananas, applesauce, flour, baking soda, and salt until well mixed.
3. Pour the batter into a small loaf pan that fits in your air fryer.
4. Cook for 30 minutes, or until a toothpick comes out clean.

5. Breakfast Burritos

 Yield:
2 servings

 Prep time:
10 minutes

 Cook time:
10 minutes

 Cooking Temperature:
400°F (200°C)

 Cooking Method:
Bake

Ingredients:
- 2 whole wheat tortillas
- 4 large eggs
- 1/2 cup black beans, rinsed
- 1/4 cup shredded cheese
- Salsa for serving

Nutritional Information

210 calories, 12g protein, 30g carbohydrates, 6g fat, 6g fiber, 0mg cholesterol, 380mg sodium, 300mg potassium.

Directions:
1. Preheat the air fryer to 400°F (200°C).
2. In a bowl, whisk eggs, and then add black beans and cheese.
3. Divide the mixture between the tortillas, wrap them tightly, and place them in the air fryer basket.
4. Cook for 10 minutes, flipping halfway through. Serve with salsa.

6. Cinnamon Apples

 Yield:
4 servings

 Prep time:
5 minutes

 Cook time:
15 minutes

 Cooking Temperature:
320°F (160°C)

 Cooking Method:
Roast

Ingredients:
- 4 apples, cored and sliced
- 1 tablespoon cinnamon
- 1 tablespoon honey or maple syrup
- 1 teaspoon lemon juice

Nutritional Information

90 calories, 0g protein, 24g carbohydrates, 0g fat, 4g fiber, 0mg cholesterol, 0mg sodium, 150mg potassium.

Directions:
1. Preheat the air fryer to 320°F (160°C).
2. In a bowl, toss apple slices with cinnamon, honey, and lemon juice.
3. Place the apple slices in the air fryer basket.
4. Cook for 15 minutes, shaking the basket halfway through.

7. Greek Yogurt Pancakes

 Yield:
4 servings

 Prep time:
10 minutes

 Cook time:
10 minutes

 Cooking Temperature:
350°F (175°C)

 Cooking Method:
Bake

Ingredients:
- 1 cup whole wheat flour
- 1 cup Greek yogurt
- 1 large egg
- 1 tablespoon honey
- 1 teaspoon baking powder

Nutritional Information

120 calories, 8g protein, 18g carbohydrates, 2g fat, 2g fiber, 40mg cholesterol, 50mg sodium, 150mg potassium.

Directions:
1. Preheat the air fryer to 350°F (175°C).
2. In a bowl, mix flour, Greek yogurt, egg, honey, and baking powder until combined.
3. Spoon the batter into silicone muffin cups or a small baking dish.
4. Cook in the air fryer for 10 minutes.

8. Veggie Frittata

 Yield:
4 servings

 Prep time:
10 minutes

 Cook time:
15 minutes

 Cooking Temperature:
350°F (175°C)

 Cooking Method:
Bake

Ingredients:
- 6 large eggs
- 1 cup chopped mixed vegetables (bell peppers, spinach, onions)
- 1/4 cup shredded cheese
- Salt and pepper to taste

Nutritional Information

130 calories, 10g protein, 3g carbohydrates, 9g fat, 1g fiber, 220mg cholesterol, 200mg sodium, 250mg potassium.

Directions:
1. Preheat the air fryer to 350°F (175°C).
2. In a bowl, whisk together eggs, mixed vegetables, cheese, salt, and pepper.
3. Pour the mixture into a greased baking dish that fits in your air fryer.
4. Cook for 15 minutes or until set in the middle.

9. French Toast Sticks

 Yield:
4 servings

 Prep time:
10 minutes

 Cook time:
10 minutes

 Cooking Temperature:
370°F (190°C)

 Cooking Method:
Bake

Ingredients:

- 4 slices whole wheat bread
- 2 large eggs
- 1/2 cup almond milk (or regular milk)
- 1 teaspoon cinnamon
- 1 teaspoon vanilla extract

Nutritional Information

150 calories, 6g protein, 22g carbohydrates, 4g fat, 3g fiber, 180mg cholesterol, 200mg sodium, 250mg potassium.

Directions:

1. Preheat the air fryer to 370°F (190°C).
2. In a bowl, whisk together eggs, milk, cinnamon, and vanilla.
3. Dip each slice of bread into the egg mixture, coating both sides, then cut into sticks.
4. Place the sticks in the air fryer basket and cook for 10 minutes, flipping halfway through.

10. Breakfast Quesadilla

 Yield:
2 servings

 Prep time:
5 minutes

 Cook time:
10 minutes

 Cooking Temperature:
400°F (200°C)

 Cooking Method:
Bake

Ingredients:

- 2 whole wheat tortillas
- 1 cup shredded cheese (cheddar or mozzarella)
- 1/2 cup cooked chicken (optional)
- 1/4 cup salsa

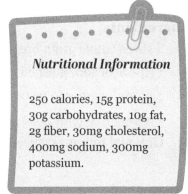

Nutritional Information

250 calories, 15g protein, 30g carbohydrates, 10g fat, 2g fiber, 30mg cholesterol, 400mg sodium, 300mg potassium.

Directions:

1. Preheat the air fryer to 400°F (200°C).
2. Place one tortilla in the air fryer basket and sprinkle half the cheese on top.
3. Add chicken (if using) and remaining cheese, then top with the second tortilla.
4. Cook for 10 minutes, flipping halfway through. Serve with salsa.

11. Chia Seed Pudding

 Yield:
2 servings

 Prep time:
5 minutes

 Cook time:
0 minutes
(Chilling time required)

 Cooking Temperature:
N/A

 Cooking Method:
N/A

Ingredients:

- 1/4 cup chia seeds
- 1 cup almond milk (or regular milk)
- 1 tablespoon honey or maple syrup
- 1/2 teaspoon vanilla extract

Nutritional Information

120 calories, 4g protein, 10g carbohydrates, 7g fat, 9g fiber, 0mg cholesterol, 20mg sodium, 40mg potassium.

Directions:

1. In a bowl, mix chia seeds, almond milk, honey, and vanilla extract.
2. Stir well to combine and let it sit for 5 minutes.
3. Stir again, then cover and refrigerate for at least 1 hour before serving.

12. Avocado Toast

 Yield:
2 servings

 Prep time:
5 minutes

 Cook time:
5 minutes

 Cooking Temperature:
350°F (175°C)

 Cooking Method:
Bake

Ingredients:

- 2 slices whole grain bread
- 1 ripe avocado, mashed
- Salt and pepper to taste
- 1 teaspoon lemon juice
- Optional toppings: sliced tomatoes, radishes, or poached eggs

Nutritional Information

220 calories, 4g protein, 28g carbohydrates, 10g fat, 8g fiber, 0mg cholesterol, 300mg sodium, 500mg potassium.

Directions:

1. Preheat the air fryer to 350°F (175°C).
2. Mash avocado with salt, pepper, and lemon juice in a bowl.
3. Spread the avocado mixture on the slices of bread.
4. Place the toast in the air fryer and cook for 5 minutes. Add optional toppings before serving.

13. Sweet Potato Hash

 Yield:
4 servings

 Prep time:
10 minutes

 Cook time:
20 minutes

 Cooking Temperature:
400°F (200°C)

 Cooking Method:
Roast

Ingredients:
- 2 medium sweet potatoes, diced
- 1 bell pepper, diced
- 1 small onion, diced
- 1 tablespoon olive oil
- Salt and pepper to taste

Nutritional Information

140 calories, 2g protein, 30g carbohydrates, 3g fat, 4g fiber, 0mg cholesterol, 190mg sodium, 300mg potassium.

Directions:
1. Preheat the air fryer to 400°F (200°C).
2. In a bowl, toss sweet potatoes, bell pepper, onion, olive oil, salt, and pepper.
3. Place the mixture in the air fryer basket.
4. Cook for 20 minutes, shaking the basket halfway through.

14. Breakfast Pita

 Yield:
2 servings

 Prep time:
5 minutes

 Cook time:
8 minutes

 Cooking Temperature:
375°F (190°C)

 Cooking Method:
Bake

Ingredients:
- 2 whole wheat pita breads
- 4 large eggs
- 1/2 cup diced tomatoes
- 1/4 cup shredded cheese
- Salt and pepper to taste

Nutritional Information

210 calories, 12g protein, 30g carbohydrates, 6g fat, 3g fiber, 220mg cholesterol, 280mg sodium, 300mg potassium.

Directions:
1. Preheat the air fryer to 375°F (190°C).
2. In a bowl, whisk together eggs, tomatoes, salt, and pepper.
3. Fill each pita bread with the egg mixture and sprinkle cheese on top.
4. Place the pitas in the air fryer and cook for 8 minutes.

15. Cottage Cheese Pancakes

 Yield:
4 servings

 Prep time:
5 minutes

 Cook time:
15 minutes

 Cooking Temperature:
360°F (180°C)

 Cooking Method:
Bake

Ingredients:
- 1 cup cottage cheese
- 4 large eggs
- 1/2 cup flour (whole wheat or all-purpose)
- 1 teaspoon vanilla extract
- 1/2 teaspoon baking powder

Nutritional Information

150 calories, 10g protein, 12g carbohydrates, 7g fat, 1g fiber, 40mg cholesterol, 300mg sodium, 250mg potassium.

Directions:
1. Preheat the air fryer to 360°F (180°C).
2. In a bowl, mix cottage cheese, eggs, flour, vanilla, and baking powder until well combined.
3. Spoon the batter into silicone muffin cups or a small baking dish.
4. Cook for 15 minutes.

16. Veggie Sausage Links

 Yield:
4 servings

 Prep time:
5 minutes

 Cook time:
10 minutes

 Cooking Temperature:
400°F (200°C)

 Cooking Method:
Fry

Ingredients:
- 8 vegetarian sausage links
- Cooking spray

Nutritional Information

180 calories, 15g protein, 4g carbohydrates, 12g fat, 2g fiber, 0mg cholesterol, 400mg sodium, 350mg potassium.

Directions:
1. Preheat the air fryer to 400°F (200°C).
2. Lightly spray the air fryer basket with cooking spray.
3. Place the sausage links in the basket in a single layer.
4. Cook for 10 minutes, flipping halfway through.

17. Cheesy Grits Casserole

 Yield:
4 servings

 Prep time:
10 minutes

 Cook time:
25 minutes

 Cooking Temperature:
350°F (175°C)

 Cooking Method:
Bake

Ingredients:

- 1 cup cooked grits
- 1 cup shredded cheese (cheddar or mozzarella)
- 2 large eggs
- 1/4 cup milk
- Salt and pepper to taste

Nutritional Information

210 calories, 10g protein, 20g carbohydrates, 10g fat, 0g fiber, 110mg cholesterol, 400mg sodium, 300mg potassium.

Directions:

1. Preheat the air fryer to 350°F (175°C).
2. In a bowl, mix cooked grits, cheese, eggs, milk, salt, and pepper until combined.
3. Pour the mixture into a small baking dish that fits in your air fryer.
4. Cook for 25 minutes or until set.

18. Ham and Egg Cups

 Yield:
4 servings

 Prep time:
5 minutes

 Cook time:
10 minutes

 Cooking Temperature:
350°F (175°C)

 Cooking Method:
Bake

Ingredients:

- 4 slices of ham
- 4 large eggs
- Salt and pepper to taste
- Optional: chopped herbs (like chives or parsley)

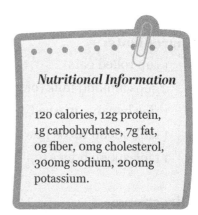

Nutritional Information

120 calories, 12g protein, 1g carbohydrates, 7g fat, 0g fiber, 0mg cholesterol, 300mg sodium, 200mg potassium.

Directions:

1. Preheat the air fryer to 350°F (175°C).
2. Place the ham slices in the cups of a silicone muffin tray, forming a cup shape.
3. Crack an egg into each ham cup and season with salt and pepper.
4. Cook for 10 minutes or until eggs are set.

19. Quinoa Breakfast Bowl

 Yield:
4 servings

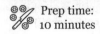 Prep time:
10 minutes

 Cook time:
15 minutes

 Cooking Temperature:
360°F (180°C)

 Cooking Method:
Bake

Ingredients:
- 1 cup cooked quinoa
- 1/2 cup almond milk (or regular milk)
- 1 tablespoon honey or maple syrup
- 1/2 teaspoon cinnamon
- 1/4 cup chopped nuts (like almonds or walnuts)

Nutritional Information

180 calories, 6g protein, 27g carbohydrates, 7g fat, 3g fiber, 0mg cholesterol, 60mg sodium, 200mg potassium.

Directions:
1. Preheat the air fryer to 360°F (180°C).
2. In a bowl, combine cooked quinoa, almond milk, honey, cinnamon, and nuts.
3. Spoon the mixture into a small baking dish that fits in your air fryer.
4. Cook for 15 minutes.

20. Chocolate Banana Oatmeal

 Yield:
2 servings

 Prep time:
5 minutes

 Cook time:
15 minutes

 Cooking Temperature:
350°F (175°C)

 Cooking Method:
Bake

Ingredients:
- 1 cup rolled oats
- 2 cups almond milk (or regular milk)
- 1 ripe banana, mashed
- 1 tablespoon cocoa powder
- 1 tablespoon honey (optional)

Nutritional Information

200 calories, 6g protein, 35g carbohydrates, 4g fat, 5g fiber, 0mg cholesterol, 80mg sodium, 300mg potassium.

Directions:
1. Preheat the air fryer to 350°F (175°C).
2. In a bowl, mix rolled oats, almond milk, mashed banana, cocoa powder, and honey until well combined.
3. Pour the mixture into a small baking dish that fits in your air fryer.
4. Cook for 15 minutes, stirring halfway through.

Chapter 3   Fast and Easy Daily Favourites

1. Lemon Garlic Chicken Thighs

 Yield:
4 servings
 Prep time:
10 minutes
 Cook time:
25 minutes
 Cooking Temperature:
400°F (200°C)
 Cooking Method:
Fry

Ingredients:

- 4 chicken thighs (boneless, skinless)
- 2 tablespoons olive oil
- 2 cloves garlic, minced
- Juice of 1 lemon
- Salt and pepper to taste

Nutritional Information

230 calories, 25g protein, 0g carbohydrates, 14g fat, 0g fiber, 90mg cholesterol, 75mg sodium, 350mg potassium.

Directions:

1. Preheat the air fryer to 400°F (200°C).
2. In a bowl, combine olive oil, garlic, lemon juice, salt, and pepper. Toss chicken thighs in the mixture.
3. Place the chicken thighs in the air fryer basket.
4. Cook for 25 minutes, flipping halfway through.

2. Zucchini Fritters

 Yield:
4 servings
 Prep time:
10 minutes
 Cook time:
15 minutes
 Cooking Temperature:
375°F (190°C)
 Cooking Method:
Bake

Ingredients:

- 2 medium zucchinis, grated
- 1/2 cup flour (whole wheat or all-purpose)
- 1/2 cup grated Parmesan cheese
- 1 egg
- Salt and pepper to taste

Nutritional Information

150 calories, 8g protein, 10g carbohydrates, 8g fat, 1g fiber, 40mg cholesterol, 200mg sodium, 180mg potassium.

Directions:

1. Preheat the air fryer to 375°F (190°C).
2. In a bowl, combine grated zucchini, flour, Parmesan, egg, salt, and pepper.
3. Form the mixture into small patties and place them in the air fryer basket.
4. Cook for 15 minutes, flipping halfway through.

3. Buffalo Cauliflower Bites

 Yield:
4 servings

 Prep time:
5 minutes

 Cook time:
15 minutes

 Cooking Temperature:
400°F (200°C)

 Cooking Method:
Fry

Ingredients:

- 1 head of cauliflower, cut into florets
- 1/2 cup buffalo sauce
- 1/2 cup breadcrumbs
- 1 tablespoon olive oil

Nutritional Information

120 calories, 4g protein, 15g carbohydrates, 5g fat, 4g fiber, 0mg cholesterol, 250mg sodium, 300mg potassium.

Directions:

1. Preheat the air fryer to 400°F (200°C).
2. Toss cauliflower florets in buffalo sauce and olive oil.
3. Coat the florets with breadcrumbs.
4. Place in the air fryer basket and cook for 15 minutes, shaking halfway through.

4. Teriyaki Salmon

 Yield:
2 servings

 Prep time:
5 minutes

 Cook time:
10 minutes

 Cooking Temperature:
400°F (200°C)

 Cooking Method:
Fry

Ingredients:

- 2 salmon fillets
- 1/4 cup teriyaki sauce
- 1 tablespoon sesame seeds
- 1 teaspoon green onions, chopped (for garnish)

Nutritional Information

300 calories, 30g protein, 10g carbohydrates, 15g fat, 0g fiber, 75mg cholesterol, 400mg sodium, 500mg potassium.

Directions:

1. Preheat the air fryer to 400°F (200°C).
2. Marinate the salmon fillets in teriyaki sauce for 5 minutes.
3. Place the fillets in the air fryer basket and sprinkle with sesame seeds.
4. Cook for 10 minutes, garnishing with green onions before serving.

5. Stuffed Bell Peppers

 Yield: 4 servings   Prep time: 10 minutes 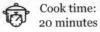 Cook time: 20 minutes 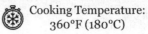 Cooking Temperature: 360°F (180°C) 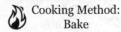 Cooking Method: Bake

Ingredients:
- 4 bell peppers, halved and seeded
- 1 cup cooked quinoa
- 1/2 cup black beans, rinsed
- 1/2 cup corn
- 1 teaspoon cumin

Nutritional Information

180 calories, 6g protein, 32g carbohydrates, 2g fat, 5g fiber, 0mg cholesterol, 300mg sodium, 400mg potassium.

Directions:
1. Preheat the air fryer to 360°F (180°C).
2. In a bowl, mix quinoa, black beans, corn, and cumin.
3. Stuff the bell pepper halves with the mixture.
4. Place stuffed peppers in the air fryer and cook for 20 minutes.

6. Turkey Meatballs

 Yield: 4 servings   Prep time: 10 minutes   Cook time: 15 minutes   Cooking Temperature: 400°F (200°C)   Cooking Method: Fry

Ingredients:
- 1 lb ground turkey
- 1/2 cup breadcrumbs
- 1/4 cup grated Parmesan cheese
- 1 egg
- 1 teaspoon Italian seasoning

Nutritional Information

180 calories, 20g protein, 10g carbohydrates, 7g fat, 0g fiber, 80mg cholesterol, 220mg sodium, 300mg potassium.

Directions:
1. Preheat the air fryer to 400°F (200°C).
2. In a bowl, combine ground turkey, breadcrumbs, Parmesan, egg, and Italian seasoning. Mix well.
3. Form into meatballs and place in the air fryer basket.
4. Cook for 15 minutes, shaking halfway through.

7. Shrimp Tacos

 Yield:
2 servings

 Prep time:
5 minutes

 Cook time:
8 minutes

 Cooking Temperature:
400°F (200°C)

 Cooking Method:
Fry

Ingredients:

- 1 lb shrimp, peeled and deveined
- 1 tablespoon olive oil
- 1 teaspoon chili powder
- 4 small corn tortillas
- Optional: salsa and avocado for topping

Nutritional Information

250 calories, 24g protein, 25g carbohydrates, 8g fat, 2g fiber, 150mg cholesterol, 360mg sodium, 280mg potassium.

Directions:

1. Preheat the air fryer to 400°F (200°C).
2. Toss shrimp with olive oil and chili powder in a bowl.
3. Place shrimp in the air fryer basket and cook for 8 minutes, shaking halfway through.
4. Serve shrimp in corn tortillas with optional toppings.

8. Broccoli and Cheese Casserole

 Yield:
4 servings

 Prep time:
10 minutes

 Cook time:
20 minutes

 Cooking Temperature:
350°F (175°C)

 Cooking Method:
Bake

Ingredients:

- 2 cups broccoli florets
- 1/2 cup shredded cheese (cheddar or mozzarella)
- 1/2 cup cooked brown rice
- 1/4 cup milk
- Salt and pepper to taste

Nutritional Information

180 calories, 8g protein, 23g carbohydrates, 7g fat, 4g fiber, 15mg cholesterol, 200mg sodium, 250mg potassium.

Directions:

1. Preheat the air fryer to 350°F (175°C).
2. In a bowl, combine broccoli, cheese, rice, milk, salt, and pepper.
3. Pour the mixture into a small baking dish that fits in the air fryer.
4. Cook for 20 minutes until the cheese is melted and bubbly.

9. Garlic Parmesan Brussels Sprouts

 Yield:
4 servings

 Prep time:
5 minutes

 Cook time:
15 minutes

 Cooking Temperature:
375°F (190°C)

 Cooking Method:
Fry

Ingredients:

- 2 cups Brussels sprouts, halved
- 1 tablespoon olive oil
- 2 tablespoons grated Parmesan cheese
- 1 teaspoon garlic powder
- Salt and pepper to taste

Nutritional Information

120 calories, 5g protein, 8g carbohydrates, 8g fat, 4g fiber, 5mg cholesterol, 150mg sodium, 300mg potassium.

Directions:

1. Preheat the air fryer to 375°F (190°C).
2. In a bowl, toss Brussels sprouts with olive oil, Parmesan, garlic powder, salt, and pepper.
3. Place in the air fryer basket.
4. Cook for 15 minutes, shaking halfway through.

10. Pesto Chicken Breasts

 Yield:
4 servings

 Prep time:
5 minutes

 Cook time:
20 minutes

 Cooking Temperature:
375°F (190°C)

 Cooking Method:
Fry

Ingredients:

- 4 boneless, skinless chicken breasts
- 1/4 cup pesto
- Salt and pepper to taste

Nutritional Information

230 calories, 27g protein, 4g carbohydrates, 12g fat, 0g fiber, 80mg cholesterol, 300mg sodium, 400mg potassium.

Directions:

1. Preheat the air fryer to 375°F (190°C).
2. Rub chicken breasts with pesto, salt, and pepper.
3. Place in the air fryer basket.
4. Cook for 20 minutes, flipping halfway through.

11. Chickpea Salad

 Yield:
4 servings

 Prep time:
5 minutes

 Cook time:
15 minutes

 Cooking Temperature:
400°F (200°C)

 Cooking Method:
Fry

Ingredients:

- 1 can (15 oz) chickpeas, drained and rinsed
- 1 tablespoon olive oil
- 1 teaspoon cumin
- Salt and pepper to taste
- 1 cup diced cucumber
- 1 cup diced tomatoes

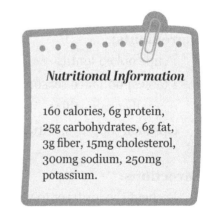

Nutritional Information

180 calories, 8g protein, 28g carbohydrates, 5g fat, 6g fiber, 0mg cholesterol, 320mg sodium, 300mg potassium.

Directions:

1. Preheat the air fryer to 400°F (200°C).
2. Toss chickpeas with olive oil, cumin, salt, and pepper.
3. Place chickpeas in the air fryer and cook for 15 minutes, shaking halfway through.
4. Serve over diced cucumber and tomatoes.

12. Eggplant Parmesan

 Yield:
4 servings

 Prep time:
10 minutes

 Cook time:
15 minutes

 Cooking Temperature:
375°F (190°C)

 Cooking Method:
Bake

Ingredients:

- 1 large eggplant, sliced into rounds
- 1 cup marinara sauce
- 1/2 cup shredded mozzarella cheese
- 1/2 cup breadcrumbs
- 1 teaspoon Italian seasoning

Nutritional Information

160 calories, 6g protein, 25g carbohydrates, 6g fat, 3g fiber, 15mg cholesterol, 300mg sodium, 250mg potassium.

Directions:

1. Preheat the air fryer to 375°F (190°C).
2. Dip eggplant slices into marinara sauce, then coat with breadcrumbs mixed with Italian seasoning.
3. Place in the air fryer basket and top with mozzarella cheese.
4. Cook for 15 minutes until golden brown.

13. Butternut Squash Soup

 Yield:
4 servings

 Prep time:
10 minutes

 Cook time:
25 minutes

 Cooking Temperature:
375°F (190°C)

 Cooking Method:
Bake

Ingredients:

- 1 medium butternut squash, peeled and cubed
- 1 tablespoon olive oil
- 1 onion, chopped
- 2 cups vegetable broth
- Salt and pepper to taste

Nutritional Information

130 calories, 3g protein, 28g carbohydrates, 2g fat, 4g fiber, 0mg cholesterol, 200mg sodium, 350mg potassium.

Directions:

1. Preheat the air fryer to 375°F (190°C).
2. Toss butternut squash and onion with olive oil, salt, and pepper.
3. Place in the air fryer basket and cook for 25 minutes, shaking halfway through.
4. Blend cooked squash and onion with vegetable broth until smooth.

14. Lentil Tacos

 Yield:
4 servings

 Prep time:
10 minutes

 Cook time:
15 minutes

 Cooking Temperature:
380°F (190°C)

 Cooking Method:
Fry

Ingredients:

- 1 cup cooked lentils
- 1 tablespoon taco seasoning
- 8 small corn tortillas
- Optional toppings: lettuce, tomato, and avocado

Nutritional Information

200 calories, 12g protein, 30g carbohydrates, 6g fat, 5g fiber, 0mg cholesterol, 250mg sodium, 300mg potassium.

Directions:

1. Preheat the air fryer to 380°F (190°C).
2. In a bowl, mix cooked lentils with taco seasoning.
3. Spoon the mixture into corn tortillas and fold.
4. Place in the air fryer and cook for 15 minutes, flipping halfway through.

15. Chicken and Broccoli

 Yield:
4 servings

 Prep time:
10 minutes

 Cook time:
15 minutes

 Cooking Temperature:
400°F (200°C)

Cooking Method:
Fry

Ingredients:
- 1 lb chicken breast, cubed
- 2 cups broccoli florets
- 2 tablespoons soy sauce
- 1 tablespoon olive oil
- 1 teaspoon garlic powder

Nutritional Information

250 calories, 30g protein,
10g carbohydrates, 10g fat,
4g fiber, 70mg cholesterol,
500mg sodium, 600mg
potassium.

Directions:
1. Preheat the air fryer to 400°F (200°C).
2. In a bowl, toss chicken, broccoli, soy sauce, olive oil, and garlic powder.
3. Place in the air fryer basket.
4. Cook for 15 minutes, shaking halfway through.

16. Spinach and Feta Stuffed Chicken

 Yield:
4 servings

 Prep time:
10 minutes

 Cook time:
25 minutes

 Cooking Temperature:
375°F (190°C)

 Cooking Method:
Fry

Ingredients:
- 4 chicken breasts
- 1 cup fresh spinach, chopped
- 1/2 cup feta cheese, crumbled
- 1 tablespoon olive oil
- Salt and pepper to taste

Nutritional Information

280 calories, 36g protein,
2g carbohydrates, 14g fat,
0g fiber, 90mg cholesterol,
80mg sodium, 400mg
potassium.

Directions:
1. Preheat the air fryer to 375°F (190°C).
2. In a bowl, mix spinach, feta, salt, and pepper.
3. Cut pockets into the chicken breasts and stuff with the spinach mixture. Rub with olive oil.
4. Place in the air fryer and cook for 25 minutes.

17. Roasted Carrots

 Yield:
4 servings

 Prep time:
5 minutes

 Cook time:
15 minutes

 Cooking Temperature:
380°F (190°C)

 Cooking Method:
Roast

Ingredients:

- 4 large carrots, sliced
- 1 tablespoon olive oil
- 1 teaspoon thyme
- Salt and pepper to taste

Directions:

1. Preheat the air fryer to 380°F (190°C).
2. In a bowl, toss carrots with olive oil, thyme, salt, and pepper.
3. Place in the air fryer basket.
4. Cook for 15 minutes, shaking halfway through.

Nutritional Information

70 calories, 1g protein, 14g carbohydrates, 3g fat, 4g fiber, 0mg cholesterol, 150mg sodium, 200mg potassium.

18. Pizza Rolls

 Yield:
6 servings

 Prep time:
5 minutes

 Cook time:
8 minutes

 Cooking Temperature:
400°F (200°C)

 Cooking Method:
Fry

Ingredients:

- 1 package (10 oz) refrigerated pizza dough
- 1/2 cup pizza sauce
- 1/2 cup shredded cheese (mozzarella or cheddar)
- 1/2 cup pepperoni or vegetables

Directions:

1. Preheat the air fryer to 400°F (200°C).
2. Roll out the pizza dough and cut into squares.
3. Place a spoonful of pizza sauce, cheese, and pepperoni/vegetables on each square and fold.
4. Place in the air fryer basket and cook for 8 minutes.

Nutritional Information

150 calories, 5g protein, 15g carbohydrates, 8g fat, 1g fiber, 10mg cholesterol, 180mg sodium, 150mg potassium.

19. Cabbage Steaks

 Yield:
4 servings

 Prep time:
5 minutes

 Cook time:
15 minutes

 Cooking Temperature:
400°F (200°C)

 Cooking Method:
Roast

Ingredients:

- 1 head of cabbage, cut into 1-inch thick steaks
- 2 tablespoons olive oil
- Salt and pepper to taste
- 1 teaspoon paprika

Nutritional Information

50 calories, 2g protein, 10g carbohydrates, 3g fat, 4g fiber, 0mg cholesterol, 60mg sodium, 300mg potassium.

Directions:

1. Preheat the air fryer to 400°F (200°C).
2. Brush cabbage steaks with olive oil and sprinkle with salt, pepper, and paprika.
3. Place in the air fryer basket.
4. Cook for 15 minutes, flipping halfway through.

20. Apple Chips

 Yield:
4 servings

 Prep time:
5 minutes

 Cook time:
15 minutes

 Cooking Temperature:
300°F (150°C)

 Cooking Method:
Bake

Ingredients:

- 2 large apples, cored and thinly sliced
- 1 teaspoon cinnamon
- 1 tablespoon lemon juice

Nutritional Information

100 calories, 0g protein, 26g carbohydrates, 0g fat, 4g fiber, 0mg cholesterol, 0mg sodium, 150mg potassium.

Directions:

1. Preheat the air fryer to 300°F (150°C).
2. Toss apple slices with lemon juice and cinnamon.
3. Arrange the apple slices in a single layer in the air fryer basket.
4. Cook for 15 minutes, shaking the basket halfway through.

Chapter 4

Best for Family

1. Chicken Fajitas

 Yield: 4 servings   Prep time: 10 minutes   Cook time: 15 minutes   Cooking Temperature: 400°F (200°C)   Cooking Method: Fry

Ingredients:

- 1 lb boneless, skinless chicken breasts, sliced
- 1 bell pepper, sliced
- 1 onion, sliced
- 2 tablespoons fajita seasoning
- 1 tablespoon olive oil

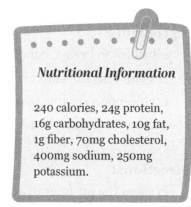

Nutritional Information

220 calories, 30g protein, 10g carbohydrates, 7g fat, 2g fiber, 70mg cholesterol, 300mg sodium, 400mg potassium.

Directions:

1. Preheat the air fryer to 400°F (200°C).
2. In a bowl, toss the chicken, bell pepper, onion, fajita seasoning, and olive oil.
3. Place the mixture in the air fryer basket.
4. Cook for 15 minutes, shaking the basket halfway through.

2. BBQ Meatballs

 Yield: 4 servings   Prep time: 5 minutes   Cook time: 12 minutes   Cooking Temperature: 400°F (200°C)   Cooking Method: Fry

Ingredients:

- 1 lb ground turkey or beef
- 1/2 cup breadcrumbs
- 1/4 cup BBQ sauce
- 1 egg
- Salt and pepper to taste

Nutritional Information

240 calories, 24g protein, 16g carbohydrates, 10g fat, 1g fiber, 70mg cholesterol, 400mg sodium, 250mg potassium.

Directions:

1. Preheat the air fryer to 400°F (200°C).
2. In a bowl, mix ground meat, breadcrumbs, BBQ sauce, egg, salt, and pepper.
3. Form into meatballs and place in the air fryer basket.
4. Cook for 12 minutes, shaking halfway through.

3. Stuffed Bell Peppers

 Yield: 4 servings   Prep time: 10 minutes   Cook time: 20 minutes   Cooking Temperature: 360°F (180°C)   Cooking Method: Bake

Ingredients:

- 4 bell peppers, halved and seeded
- 1 cup cooked rice (brown or white)
- 1 cup black beans, rinsed
- 1 cup corn
- 1 teaspoon cumin

Directions:

1. Preheat the air fryer to 360°F (180°C).
2. In a bowl, combine cooked rice, black beans, corn, and cumin.
3. Stuff the bell pepper halves with the mixture.
4. Place in the air fryer and cook for 20 minutes.

Nutritional Information

190 calories, 7g protein, 36g carbohydrates, 2g fat, 7g fiber, 0mg cholesterol, 220mg sodium, 400mg potassium.

4. Teriyaki Chicken

 Yield: 4 servings   Prep time: 10 minutes   Cook time: 15 minutes   Cooking Temperature: 400°F (200°C)   Cooking Method: Fry

Ingredients:

- 1 lb chicken breast, cubed
- 1/4 cup teriyaki sauce
- 1 tablespoon sesame seeds
- 1 teaspoon green onions, chopped (for garnish)

Directions:

1. Preheat the air fryer to 400°F (200°C).
2. Marinate the chicken cubes in teriyaki sauce for 10 minutes.
3. Place the chicken in the air fryer basket and sprinkle with sesame seeds.
4. Cook for 15 minutes, garnishing with green onions before serving.

Nutritional Information

230 calories, 29g protein, 8g carbohydrates, 8g fat, 0g fiber, 70mg cholesterol, 320mg sodium, 420mg potassium.

5. Sweet Potato Fries

 Yield:
4 servings

 Prep time:
10 minutes

 Cook time:
20 minutes

 Cooking Temperature:
400°F (200°C)

 Cooking Method:
Fry

Ingredients:

- 2 large sweet potatoes, cut into fries
- 1 tablespoon olive oil
- 1 teaspoon paprika
- Salt to taste

Directions:

1. Preheat the air fryer to 400°F (200°C).
2. In a bowl, toss sweet potato fries with olive oil, paprika, and salt.
3. Place in the air fryer basket in a single layer.
4. Cook for 20 minutes, shaking halfway through.

Nutritional Information

160 calories, 2g protein, 37g carbohydrates, 5g fat, 6g fiber, 0mg cholesterol, 200mg sodium, 400mg potassium.

6. Salmon with Lemon

 Yield:
2 servings

 Prep time:
5 minutes

 Cook time:
10 minutes

 Cooking Temperature:
400°F (200°C)

 Cooking Method:
Fry

Ingredients:

- 2 salmon fillets
- 1 tablespoon olive oil
- Juice of 1 lemon
- Salt and pepper to taste

Directions:

1. Preheat the air fryer to 400°F (200°C).
2. Brush salmon with olive oil, lemon juice, salt, and pepper.
3. Place in the air fryer basket.
4. Cook for 10 minutes.

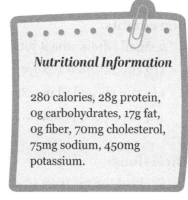

Nutritional Information

280 calories, 28g protein, 0g carbohydrates, 17g fat, 0g fiber, 70mg cholesterol, 75mg sodium, 450mg potassium.

7. Broccoli and Cheese Casserole

 Yield:
4 servings

 Prep time:
5 minutes

 Cook time:
15 minutes

 Cooking Temperature:
350°F (175°C)

 Cooking Method:
Bake

Ingredients:
- 2 cups broccoli florets
- 1/2 cup shredded cheddar cheese
- 1/2 cup cooked brown rice
- 1/4 cup milk
- Salt and pepper to taste

Nutritional Information

190 calories, 8g protein, 23g carbohydrates, 8g fat, 3g fiber, 20mg cholesterol, 250mg sodium, 300mg potassium.

Directions:
1. Preheat the air fryer to 350°F (175°C).
2. In a bowl, combine broccoli, cheese, rice, milk, salt, and pepper.
3. Pour into a small baking dish that fits in the air fryer.
4. Cook for 15 minutes until cheese is melted.

8. Mini Pizza

 Yield:
2 servings

 Prep time:
5 minutes

 Cook time:
10 minutes

 Cooking Temperature:
400°F (200°C)

 Cooking Method:
Fry

Ingredients:
- 2 small whole wheat pita breads
- 1/2 cup marinara sauce
- 1/2 cup shredded mozzarella cheese
- 1/4 cup sliced pepperoni or vegetables

Nutritional Information

300 calories, 12g protein, 36g carbohydrates, 12g fat, 2g fiber, 30mg cholesterol, 480mg sodium, 300mg potassium.

Directions:
1. Preheat the air fryer to 400°F (200°C).
2. Spread marinara sauce on each pita bread and top with cheese and pepperoni/vegetables.
3. Place in the air fryer basket.
4. Cook for 10 minutes until cheese is melted.

9. Egg and Veggie Breakfast Bowls

 Yield:
4 servings

 Prep time:
10 minutes

 Cook time:
15 minutes

 Cooking Temperature:
350°F (175°C)

 Cooking Method:
Bake

Ingredients:

- 8 large eggs
- 1 cup mixed vegetables (spinach, bell peppers, onions)
- 1/2 teaspoon salt
- 1/4 teaspoon black pepper

Directions:

1. Preheat the air fryer to 350°F (175°C).
2. In a bowl, whisk together eggs, mixed vegetables, salt, and pepper.
3. Pour the mixture into silicone muffin cups or a small baking dish.
4. Cook for 15 minutes or until set.

Nutritional Information

120 calories, 10g protein, 2g carbohydrates, 8g fat, 0g fiber, 186mg cholesterol, 200mg sodium, 150mg potassium.

10. Pork Chops

 Yield:
4 servings

 Prep time:
5 minutes

 Cook time:
12 minutes

 Cooking Temperature:
400°F (200°C)

 Cooking Method:
Fry

Ingredients:

- 4 boneless pork chops
- 1 tablespoon olive oil
- 1 teaspoon garlic powder
- Salt and pepper to taste

Directions:

1. Preheat the air fryer to 400°F (200°C).
2. Rub pork chops with olive oil, garlic powder, salt, and pepper.
3. Place in the air fryer basket.
4. Cook for 12 minutes, flipping halfway through.

Nutritional Information

220 calories, 30g protein, 0g carbohydrates, 10g fat, 0g fiber, 80mg cholesterol, 60mg sodium, 400mg potassium.

11. Vegetable Samosas

 Yield:
4 servings

 Prep time:
15 minutes

 Cook time:
15 minutes

 Cooking Temperature:
380°F (190°C)

 Cooking Method:
Fry

Ingredients:
- 2 cups mixed vegetables (peas, carrots, potatoes), cooked
- 1 teaspoon garam masala
- 1 tablespoon olive oil
- 4 wonton wrappers

Nutritional Information

160 calories, 5g protein, 25g carbohydrates, 5g fat, 4g fiber, 0mg cholesterol, 180mg sodium, 220mg potassium.

Directions:
1. Preheat the air fryer to 380°F (190°C).
2. In a bowl, mix cooked vegetables with garam masala and olive oil.
3. Fill each wonton wrapper with the vegetable mixture and fold.
4. Place in the air fryer and cook for 15 minutes, turning halfway.

12. Quinoa Salad

 Yield:
4 servings

 Prep time:
5 minutes

 Cook time:
0 minutes
(Chilling time required)

 Cooking Temperature:
N/A

 Cooking Method:
N/A

Ingredients:
- 1 cup cooked quinoa
- 1 cup cherry tomatoes, halved
- 1/2 cup cucumber, diced
- 1/4 cup parsley, chopped
- 2 tablespoons lemon juice

Nutritional Information

150 calories, 5g protein, 30g carbohydrates, 2g fat, 3g fiber, 0mg cholesterol, 10mg sodium, 250mg potassium.

Directions:
1. In a bowl, mix cooked quinoa, cherry tomatoes, cucumber, parsley, and lemon juice.
2. Chill in the refrigerator for at least 30 minutes before serving.

13. Honey Garlic Chicken Wings

 Yield: 4 servings Prep time: 5 minutes Cook time: 25 minutes Cooking Temperature: 400°F (200°C) Cooking Method: Fry

Ingredients:

- 2 lbs chicken wings
- 1/4 cup honey
- 2 tablespoons soy sauce
- 2 cloves garlic, minced

Nutritional Information

300 calories, 25g protein, 12g carbohydrates, 18g fat, 0g fiber, 70mg cholesterol, 500mg sodium, 300mg potassium.

Directions:

1. Preheat the air fryer to 400°F (200°C).
2. In a bowl, mix honey, soy sauce, and garlic. Toss chicken wings in the mixture.
3. Place wings in the air fryer basket.
4. Cook for 25 minutes, flipping halfway through.

14. Cabbage and Sausage Skillet

 Yield: 4 servings Prep time: 10 minutes Cook time: 20 minutes Cooking Temperature: 380°F (190°C) Cooking Method: Fry

Ingredients:

- 1/2 head of cabbage, chopped
- 1 lb turkey sausage, sliced
- 1 tablespoon olive oil
- Salt and pepper to taste

Nutritional Information

220 calories, 18g protein, 10g carbohydrates, 13g fat, 3g fiber, 60mg cholesterol, 600mg sodium, 500mg potassium.

Directions:

1. Preheat the air fryer to 380°F (190°C).
2. Toss chopped cabbage, sausage, olive oil, salt, and pepper in a bowl.
3. Place in the air fryer basket.
4. Cook for 20 minutes, shaking halfway through.

15. Cheesy Broccoli Rice

 Yield:
4 servings

 Prep time:
10 minutes

 Cook time:
15 minutes

 Cooking Temperature:
350°F (175°C)

 Cooking Method:
Bake

Ingredients:
- 2 cups cooked brown rice
- 1 cup broccoli florets
- 1/2 cup shredded cheddar cheese
- 1/4 cup milk
- Salt and pepper to taste

Nutritional Information

210 calories, 7g protein, 30g carbohydrates, 8g fat, 3g fiber, 15mg cholesterol, 350mg sodium, 400mg potassium.

Directions:
1. Preheat the air fryer to 350°F (175°C).
2. In a bowl, mix cooked rice, broccoli, cheese, milk, salt, and pepper.
3. Pour the mixture into a small baking dish that fits in the air fryer.
4. Cook for 15 minutes until the cheese is melted.

16. Turkey and Spinach Stuffed Peppers

 Yield:
4 servings

 Prep time:
10 minutes

 Cook time:
20 minutes

 Cooking Temperature:
360°F (180°C)

 Cooking Method:
Bake

Ingredients:
- 4 bell peppers, halved and seeded
- 1 lb ground turkey
- 1 cup fresh spinach, chopped
- 1/2 cup diced tomatoes
- 1 teaspoon Italian seasoning

Nutritional Information

230 calories, 30g protein, 15g carbohydrates, 5g fat, 3g fiber, 70mg cholesterol, 400mg sodium, 450mg potassium.

Directions:
1. Preheat the air fryer to 360°F (180°C).
2. In a bowl, combine ground turkey, spinach, diced tomatoes, and Italian seasoning.
3. Stuff the bell pepper halves with the mixture.
4. Place in the air fryer and cook for 20 minutes.

17. Vegetable Quesadillas

Yield: 4 servings | Prep time: 5 minutes | Cook time: 10 minutes | Cooking Temperature: 375°F (190°C) | Cooking Method: Bake

Ingredients:

- 4 whole wheat tortillas
- 1 cup mixed vegetables (bell peppers, onions, mushrooms)
- 1 cup shredded cheese (mozzarella or cheddar)
- Cooking spray

Nutritional Information

250 calories, 12g protein, 30g carbohydrates, 10g fat, 3g fiber, 20mg cholesterol, 400mg sodium, 300mg potassium.

Directions:

1. Preheat the air fryer to 375°F (190°C).
2. Place tortillas on a flat surface, layer with cheese and mixed vegetables, and fold.
3. Lightly spray the air fryer basket with cooking spray.
4. Place quesadillas in the air fryer and cook for 10 minutes, flipping halfway through.

18. Spinach Artichoke Dip

Yield: 4 servings | Prep time: 10 minutes | Cook time: 15 minutes | Cooking Temperature: 350°F (175°C) | Cooking Method: Bake

Ingredients:

- 1 cup frozen spinach, thawed and drained
- 1 cup canned artichoke hearts, chopped
- 1/2 cup cream cheese
- 1/4 cup Greek yogurt
- 1/2 cup shredded mozzarella cheese

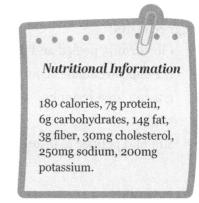

Nutritional Information

180 calories, 7g protein, 6g carbohydrates, 14g fat, 3g fiber, 30mg cholesterol, 250mg sodium, 200mg potassium.

Directions:

1. Preheat the air fryer to 350°F (175°C).
2. In a bowl, mix spinach, artichoke hearts, cream cheese, Greek yogurt, and mozzarella until combined.
3. Spread the mixture into a small baking dish that fits in the air fryer.
4. Cook for 15 minutes until hot and bubbly.

19. Honey Mustard Chicken Drumsticks

 Yield:
4 servings

 Prep time:
5 minutes

 Cook time:
25 minutes

 Cooking Temperature:
400°F (200°C)

 Cooking Method:
Fry

Ingredients:
- 8 chicken drumsticks
- 1/4 cup honey
- 1/4 cup Dijon mustard
- Salt and pepper to taste

Directions:
1. Preheat the air fryer to 400°F (200°C).
2. In a bowl, mix honey, Dijon mustard, salt, and pepper. Toss chicken drumsticks in the mixture.
3. Place drumsticks in the air fryer basket.
4. Cook for 25 minutes, turning halfway.

Nutritional Information

320 calories, 25g protein, 16g carbohydrates, 15g fat, 0g fiber, 90mg cholesterol, 300mg sodium, 400mg potassium.

20. Coconut Shrimp

 Yield:
4 servings

 Prep time:
10 minutes

 Cook time:
12 minutes

 Cooking Temperature:
400°F (200°C)

 Cooking Method:
Fry

Ingredients:
- 1 lb shrimp, peeled and deveined
- 1/2 cup shredded coconut
- 1/2 cup breadcrumbs
- 1 egg
- Salt and pepper to taste

Directions:
1. Preheat the air fryer to 400°F (200°C).
2. Dip shrimp in beaten egg, then coat with a mixture of shredded coconut and breadcrumbs.
3. Place shrimp in the air fryer basket.
4. Cook for 12 minutes, flipping halfway through.

Nutritional Information

250 calories, 20g protein, 18g carbohydrates, 10g fat, 2g fiber, 200mg cholesterol, 350mg sodium, 280mg potassium.

Chapter 5

Best for TWO

1. Lemon Herb Chicken Breasts

 Yield:
2 servings

 Prep time:
5 minutes

 Cook time:
20 minutes

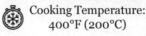 Cooking Temperature:
400°F (200°C)

 Cooking Method:
Fry

Ingredients:

- 2 boneless, skinless chicken breasts
- 1 tablespoon olive oil
- Juice of 1 lemon
- 1 teaspoon dried oregano
- Salt and pepper to taste

Nutritional Information

220 calories, 30g protein,
0g carbohydrates, 10g fat,
0g fiber, 80mg cholesterol,
75mg sodium, 450mg
potassium.

Directions:

1. Preheat the air fryer to 400°F (200°C).
2. In a bowl, mix olive oil, lemon juice, oregano, salt, and pepper. Coat chicken breasts in the mixture.
3. Place the chicken in the air fryer basket.
4. Cook for 20 minutes, flipping halfway through.

2. Garlic Parmesan Cauliflower

 Yield:
2 servings

 Prep time:
5 minutes

 Cook time:
15 minutes

 Cooking Temperature:
375°F (190°C)

 Cooking Method:
Fry

Ingredients:

- 1 small head cauliflower, cut into florets
- 1 tablespoon olive oil
- 2 tablespoons grated Parmesan cheese
- 1 teaspoon garlic powder
- Salt and pepper to taste

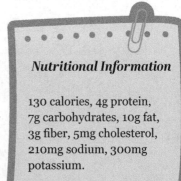

Nutritional Information

130 calories, 4g protein,
7g carbohydrates, 10g fat,
3g fiber, 5mg cholesterol,
210mg sodium, 300mg
potassium.

Directions:

1. Preheat the air fryer to 375°F (190°C).
2. In a bowl, toss cauliflower florets with olive oil, Parmesan, garlic powder, salt, and pepper.
3. Place in the air fryer basket.
4. Cook for 15 minutes, shaking halfway through.

3. Shrimp Skewers

 Yield:
2 servings

 Prep time:
10 minutes

 Cook time:
8 minutes

 Cooking Temperature:
400°F (200°C)

 Cooking Method:
Fry

Ingredients:

- 1 lb shrimp, peeled and deveined
- 1 tablespoon olive oil
- 1 teaspoon paprika
- Salt and pepper to taste
- Skewers

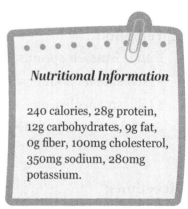

Nutritional Information

200 calories, 24g protein, 2g carbohydrates, 10g fat, 0g fiber, 200mg cholesterol, 400mg sodium, 300mg potassium.

Directions:

1. Preheat the air fryer to 400°F (200°C).
2. Toss shrimp with olive oil, paprika, salt, and pepper.
3. Thread shrimp onto skewers.
4. Place skewers in the air fryer and cook for 8 minutes, flipping halfway through.

4. Turkey Burgers

 Yield:
2 servings

 Prep time:
10 minutes

 Cook time:
15 minutes

 Cooking Temperature:
375°F (190°C)

 Cooking Method:
Fry

Ingredients:

- 1 lb ground turkey
- 1/4 cup breadcrumbs
- 1 egg
- 1 teaspoon onion powder
- Salt and pepper to taste

Nutritional Information

240 calories, 28g protein, 12g carbohydrates, 9g fat, 0g fiber, 100mg cholesterol, 350mg sodium, 280mg potassium.

Directions:

1. Preheat the air fryer to 375°F (190°C).
2. In a bowl, mix ground turkey, breadcrumbs, egg, onion powder, salt, and pepper.
3. Form into two patties and place in the air fryer basket.
4. Cook for 15 minutes, flipping halfway through.

5. Stuffed Mushrooms

 Yield:
2 servings

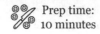 Prep time:
10 minutes

 Cook time:
10 minutes

 Cooking Temperature:
350°F (175°C)

 Cooking Method:
Bake

Ingredients:

- 12 large mushrooms, stems removed
- 1/2 cup cream cheese, softened
- 1/4 cup shredded cheese (your choice)
- 1 tablespoon fresh herbs (like parsley or thyme)
- Salt and pepper to taste

Nutritional Information

200 calories, 8g protein, 10g carbohydrates, 14g fat, 1g fiber, 40mg cholesterol, 300mg sodium, 250mg potassium.

Directions:

1. Preheat the air fryer to 350°F (175°C).
2. In a bowl, mix cream cheese, shredded cheese, herbs, salt, and pepper.
3. Stuff each mushroom cap with the mixture.
4. Place stuffed mushrooms in the air fryer and cook for 10 minutes.

6. Balsamic Brussels Sprouts

 Yield:
2 servings

 Prep time:
5 minutes

 Cook time:
15 minutes

 Cooking Temperature:
375°F (190°C)

 Cooking Method:
Fry

Ingredients:

- 2 cups Brussels sprouts, halved
- 1 tablespoon balsamic vinegar
- 1 tablespoon olive oil
- Salt and pepper to taste

Nutritional Information

130 calories, 4g protein, 10g carbohydrates, 8g fat, 4g fiber, 0mg cholesterol, 160mg sodium, 300mg potassium.

Directions:

1. Preheat the air fryer to 375°F (190°C).
2. In a bowl, toss Brussels sprouts with balsamic vinegar, olive oil, salt, and pepper.
3. Place in the air fryer basket.
4. Cook for 15 minutes, shaking halfway through.

7. BBQ Chicken Drumsticks

 Yield:
2 servings

 Prep time:
5 minutes

 Cook time:
25 minutes

 Cooking Temperature:
400°F (200°C)

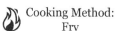 Cooking Method:
Fry

Ingredients:
- 4 chicken drumsticks
- 1/4 cup BBQ sauce
- Salt and pepper to taste

Directions:
1. Preheat the air fryer to 400°F (200°C).
2. Season drumsticks with salt and pepper, then brush with BBQ sauce.
3. Place in the air fryer basket.
4. Cook for 25 minutes, turning halfway and basting with more BBQ sauce if desired.

Nutritional Information

250 calories, 24g protein, 8g carbohydrates, 14g fat, 0g fiber, 90mg cholesterol, 300mg sodium, 350mg potassium.

8. Spinach and Feta Stuffed Chicken

 Yield:
2 servings

 Prep time:
10 minutes

 Cook time:
25 minutes

 Cooking Temperature:
375°F (190°C)

 Cooking Method:
Fry

Ingredients:
- 2 boneless, skinless chicken breasts
- 1/2 cup fresh spinach, chopped
- 1/4 cup feta cheese, crumbled
- 1 tablespoon olive oil
- Salt and pepper to taste

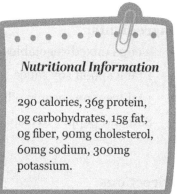

Nutritional Information

290 calories, 36g protein, 0g carbohydrates, 15g fat, 0g fiber, 90mg cholesterol, 60mg sodium, 300mg potassium.

Directions:
1. Preheat the air fryer to 375°F (190°C).
2. In a bowl, mix spinach, feta, salt, and pepper.
3. Cut pockets in the chicken breasts and stuff with the mixture. Rub with olive oil.
4. Place in the air fryer and cook for 25 minutes.

9. Eggplant Fries

 Yield:
2 servings

 Prep time:
10 minutes

 Cook time:
15 minutes

 Cooking Temperature:
400°F (200°C)

 Cooking Method:
Fry

Ingredients:

- 1 large eggplant, cut into fries
- 1/4 cup breadcrumbs
- 1/4 cup grated Parmesan cheese
- 1 egg, beaten
- Salt and pepper to taste

Nutritional Information

180 calories, 5g protein, 24g carbohydrates, 7g fat, 5g fiber, 0mg cholesterol, 250mg sodium, 350mg potassium.

Directions:

1. Preheat the air fryer to 400°F (200°C).
2. Dip eggplant fries in beaten egg, then coat with a mixture of breadcrumbs, Parmesan, salt, and pepper.
3. Place in the air fryer basket.
4. Cook for 15 minutes, shaking halfway through.

10. Vegetable Stir-Fry

 Yield:
2 servings

 Prep time:
5 minutes

 Cook time:
10 minutes

 Cooking Temperature:
400°F (200°C)

 Cooking Method:
Fry

Ingredients:

- 2 cups mixed vegetables (broccoli, bell peppers, carrots)
- 1 tablespoon soy sauce
- 1 tablespoon sesame oil
- Salt and pepper to taste

Nutritional Information

100 calories, 3g protein, 15g carbohydrates, 4g fat, 5g fiber, 0mg cholesterol, 200mg sodium, 300mg potassium.

Directions:

1. Preheat the air fryer to 400°F (200°C).
2. In a bowl, toss mixed vegetables with soy sauce, sesame oil, salt, and pepper.
3. Place in the air fryer basket.
4. Cook for 10 minutes, shaking halfway through.

11. Chicken and Veggie Bowls

 Yield: 2 servings   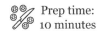 Prep time: 10 minutes   Cook time: 15 minutes   Cooking Temperature: 380°F (190°C)   Cooking Method: Fry

Ingredients:

- 1 lb chicken breast, cubed
- 2 cups mixed vegetables (zucchini, bell peppers, carrots)
- 1 tablespoon olive oil
- 1 teaspoon Italian seasoning

Directions:

1. Preheat the air fryer to 380°F (190°C).
2. Toss chicken and mixed vegetables with olive oil and Italian seasoning in a bowl.
3. Place in the air fryer basket.
4. Cook for 15 minutes, shaking halfway through.

Nutritional Information

250 calories, 30g protein, 10g carbohydrates, 10g fat, 2g fiber, 70mg cholesterol, 150mg sodium, 400mg potassium.

12. Pesto Pasta

 Yield: 2 servings   Prep time: 10 minutes   Cook time: 12 minutes   Cooking Temperature: 350°F (175°C)   Cooking Method: Bake

Ingredients:

- 2 cups cooked pasta (whole wheat or regular)
- 1/4 cup pesto
- 1/4 cup cherry tomatoes, halved
- 1/4 cup grated Parmesan cheese

Directions:

1. Preheat the air fryer to 350°F (175°C).
2. In a bowl, mix cooked pasta, pesto, and cherry tomatoes.
3. Pour the mixture into a small baking dish that fits in the air fryer.
4. Top with Parmesan cheese and cook for 12 minutes.

Nutritional Information

300 calories, 10g protein, 45g carbohydrates, 10g fat, 3g fiber, 10mg cholesterol, 250mg sodium, 350mg potassium.

13. Bacon-Wrapped Asparagus

 Yield:
2 servings

 Prep time:
5 minutes

 Cook time:
10 minutes

 Cooking Temperature:
400°F (200°C)

 Cooking Method:
Fry

Ingredients:

- 1 bunch asparagus, trimmed
- 4 slices turkey bacon
- Salt and pepper to taste

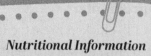

Nutritional Information

150 calories, 10g protein, 8g carbohydrates, 10g fat, 3g fiber, 20mg cholesterol, 250mg sodium, 300mg potassium.

Directions:

1. Preheat the air fryer to 400°F (200°C).
2. Wrap each asparagus spear with a slice of bacon and season with salt and pepper.
3. Place in the air fryer basket.
4. Cook for 10 minutes until bacon is crispy.

14. Thai Chicken Lettuce Wraps

 Yield:
2 servings

 Prep time:
10 minutes

 Cook time:
12 minutes

 Cooking Temperature:
380°F (190°C)

 Cooking Method:
Fry

Ingredients:

- 1 lb ground chicken
- 1/4 cup soy sauce
- 2 tablespoons peanut butter
- 1 teaspoon ginger, minced
- Butter lettuce leaves for wrapping

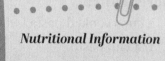

Nutritional Information

220 calories, 24g protein, 6g carbohydrates, 10g fat, 1g fiber, 70mg cholesterol, 450mg sodium, 300mg potassium.

Directions:

1. Preheat the air fryer to 380°F (190°C).
2. In a bowl, mix ground chicken, soy sauce, peanut butter, and ginger.
3. Place the mixture in the air fryer basket and cook for 12 minutes, breaking up the chicken halfway through.
4. Serve in lettuce leaves.

15. Cheese-Stuffed Peppers

 Yield:
2 servings

 Prep time:
5 minutes

 Cook time:
15 minutes

 Cooking Temperature:
360°F (180°C)

 Cooking Method:
Bake

Ingredients:

- 2 bell peppers, halved and seeded
- 1/2 cup ricotta cheese
- 1/4 cup shredded mozzarella cheese
- Salt and pepper to taste

Directions:

1. Preheat the air fryer to 360°F (180°C).
2. In a bowl, mix ricotta, mozzarella, salt, and pepper.
3. Stuff each bell pepper half with the cheese mixture.
4. Place in the air fryer and cook for 15 minutes.

Nutritional Information

180 calories, 9g protein, 10g carbohydrates, 11g fat, 2g fiber, 25mg cholesterol, 300mg sodium, 200mg potassium.

16. Tomato Basil Chicken

 Yield:
2 servings

 Prep time:
5 minutes

 Cook time:
15 minutes

 Cooking Temperature:
400°F (200°C)

 Cooking Method:
Fry

Ingredients:

- 2 boneless, skinless chicken breasts
- 1/2 cup cherry tomatoes, halved
- 1 tablespoon olive oil
- 1 teaspoon dried basil
- Salt and pepper to taste

Directions:

1. Preheat the air fryer to 400°F (200°C).
2. In a bowl, mix chicken breasts with cherry tomatoes, olive oil, basil, salt, and pepper.
3. Place the mixture in the air fryer basket.
4. Cook for 15 minutes, flipping the chicken halfway through.

Nutritional Information

240 calories, 30g protein, 8g carbohydrates, 10g fat, 2g fiber, 60mg cholesterol, 300mg sodium, 350mg potassium.

17. Honey Garlic Pork Tenderloin

 Yield:
2 servings

 Prep time:
5 minutes

 Cook time:
20 minutes

 Cooking Temperature:
400°F (200°C)

 Cooking Method:
Fry

Ingredients:

- 1 lb pork tenderloin
- 1/4 cup honey
- 2 tablespoons soy sauce
- 2 cloves garlic, minced
- Salt and pepper to taste

Directions:

1. Preheat the air fryer to 400°F (200°C).
2. In a bowl, mix honey, soy sauce, garlic, salt, and pepper. Coat the pork tenderloin with the mixture.
3. Place the tenderloin in the air fryer basket.
4. Cook for 20 minutes, flipping halfway through.

Nutritional Information

300 calories, 35g protein, 25g carbohydrates, 7g fat, 0g fiber, 80mg cholesterol, 500mg sodium, 450mg potassium.

18. Lemon Garlic Green Beans

 Yield:
2 servings

 Prep time:
5 minutes

 Cook time:
10 minutes

 Cooking Temperature:
400°F (200°C)

 Cooking Method:
Fry

Ingredients:

- 2 cups green beans, trimmed
- 1 tablespoon olive oil
- 1 teaspoon garlic powder
- Juice of 1 lemon
- Salt and pepper to taste

Directions:

1. Preheat the air fryer to 400°F (200°C).
2. Toss green beans with olive oil, garlic powder, lemon juice, salt, and pepper in a bowl.
3. Place in the air fryer basket.
4. Cook for 10 minutes, shaking halfway through.

Nutritional Information

90 calories, 3g protein, 12g carbohydrates, 4g fat, 4g fiber, 0mg cholesterol, 40mg sodium, 250mg potassium.

19. Spicy Chickpeas

 Yield:
2 servings

 Prep time:
5 minutes

 Cook time:
15 minutes

 Cooking Temperature:
400°F (200°C)

 Cooking Method:
Fry

Ingredients:
- 1 can (15 oz) chickpeas, drained and rinsed
- 1 tablespoon olive oil
- 1 teaspoon chili powder
- Salt to taste

Nutritional Information

150 calories, 7g protein, 25g carbohydrates, 5g fat, 7g fiber, 0mg cholesterol, 300mg sodium, 400mg potassium.

Directions:
1. Preheat the air fryer to 400°F (200°C).
2. Toss chickpeas with olive oil, chili powder, and salt in a bowl.
3. Place in the air fryer basket.
4. Cook for 15 minutes, shaking halfway through.

20. Coconut Curry Chicken

 Yield:
2 servings

 Prep time:
10 minutes

 Cook time:
20 minutes

 Cooking Temperature:
375°F (190°C)

 Cooking Method:
Fry

Ingredients:
- 1 lb chicken thighs, cubed
- 1/4 cup coconut milk
- 2 tablespoons curry powder
- Salt to taste

Nutritional Information

300 calories, 28g protein, 8g carbohydrates, 18g fat, 0g fiber, 90mg cholesterol, 350mg sodium, 400mg potassium.

Directions:
1. Preheat the air fryer to 375°F (190°C).
2. In a bowl, combine chicken, coconut milk, curry powder, and salt.
3. Place the mixture in the air fryer basket.
4. Cook for 20 minutes, shaking halfway through.

Chapter 6

Fish and Seafood

1. Lemon Garlic Salmon

 Yield: 2 servings   Prep time: 5 minutes   Cook time: 10 minutes   Cooking Temperature: 400°F (200°C)   Cooking Method: Fry

Ingredients:

- 2 salmon fillets
- 1 tablespoon olive oil
- Juice of 1 lemon
- 2 cloves garlic, minced
- Salt and pepper to taste

Nutritional Information

280 calories, 30g protein, 0g carbohydrates, 15g fat, 0g fiber, 75mg cholesterol, 70mg sodium, 450mg potassium.

Directions:

1. Preheat the air fryer to 400°F (200°C).
2. In a bowl, mix olive oil, lemon juice, garlic, salt, and pepper. Coat the salmon fillets in the mixture.
3. Place salmon in the air fryer basket.
4. Cook for 10 minutes.

2. Spicy Shrimp Tacos

 Yield: 2 servings   Prep time: 10 minutes   Cook time: 8 minutes   Cooking Temperature: 400°F (200°C)   Cooking Method: Fry

Ingredients:

- 1 lb shrimp, peeled and deveined
- 1 tablespoon olive oil
- 1 teaspoon chili powder
- Salt and pepper to taste
- 4 small corn tortillas

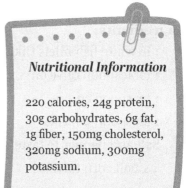

Nutritional Information

220 calories, 24g protein, 30g carbohydrates, 6g fat, 1g fiber, 150mg cholesterol, 320mg sodium, 300mg potassium.

Directions:

1. Preheat the air fryer to 400°F (200°C).
2. Toss shrimp with olive oil, chili powder, salt, and pepper.
3. Place shrimp in the air fryer basket.
4. Cook for 8 minutes, then serve in corn tortillas.

3. Cod with Lemon Dill Sauce

 Yield:
2 servings
 Prep time:
5 minutes
 Cook time:
12 minutes
 Cooking Temperature:
375°F (190°C)
 Cooking Method:
Fry

Ingredients:

- 2 cod fillets
- 1 tablespoon olive oil
- 1 teaspoon dill weed
- Juice of 1 lemon
- Salt and pepper to taste

Nutritional Information

220 calories, 30g protein, 0g carbohydrates, 10g fat, 0g fiber, 75mg cholesterol, 60mg sodium, 400mg potassium.

Directions:

1. Preheat the air fryer to 375°F (190°C).
2. Brush cod fillets with olive oil and sprinkle with dill, lemon juice, salt, and pepper.
3. Place in the air fryer basket.
4. Cook for 12 minutes.

4. Fish Tacos

 Yield:
2 servings
 Prep time:
10 minutes
 Cook time:
10 minutes
 Cooking Temperature:
400°F (200°C)
 Cooking Method:
Fry

Ingredients:

- 1 lb white fish fillets (like tilapia or haddock)
- 1 tablespoon olive oil
- 1 teaspoon cumin
- 1 teaspoon paprika
- Salt and pepper to taste
- 4 small corn tortillas

Nutritional Information

210 calories, 25g protein, 30g carbohydrates, 5g fat, 2g fiber, 50mg cholesterol, 200mg sodium, 350mg potassium.

Directions:

1. Preheat the air fryer to 400°F (200°C).
2. In a bowl, mix olive oil, cumin, paprika, salt, and pepper. Coat the fish fillets in the mixture.
3. Place fish in the air fryer basket.
4. Cook for 10 minutes, then serve in corn tortillas.

5. Garlic Butter Shrimp

 Yield:
2 servings

 Prep time:
5 minutes

 Cook time:
7 minutes

 Cooking Temperature:
400°F (200°C)

 Cooking Method:
Fry

Ingredients:

- 1 lb shrimp, peeled and deveined
- 2 tablespoons butter, melted
- 2 cloves garlic, minced
- Salt and pepper to taste
- 1 tablespoon fresh parsley, chopped (for garnish)

Nutritional Information

240 calories, 24g protein, 0g carbohydrates, 16g fat, 0g fiber, 170mg cholesterol, 180mg sodium, 300mg potassium.

Directions:

1. Preheat the air fryer to 400°F (200°C).
2. In a bowl, mix shrimp with melted butter, garlic, salt, and pepper.
3. Place shrimp in the air fryer basket.
4. Cook for 7 minutes and garnish with parsley before serving.

6. Teriyaki Salmon

 Yield:
2 servings

 Prep time:
5 minutes

 Cook time:
10 minutes

 Cooking Temperature:
400°F (200°C)

 Cooking Method:
Fry

Ingredients:

- 2 salmon fillets
- 1/4 cup teriyaki sauce
- 1 teaspoon sesame seeds (optional)
- 1 teaspoon green onions, chopped (for garnish)

Nutritional Information

280 calories, 30g protein, 10g carbohydrates, 10g fat, 0g fiber, 70mg cholesterol, 400mg sodium, 450mg potassium.

Directions:

1. Preheat the air fryer to 400°F (200°C).
2. Marinate salmon fillets in teriyaki sauce for 5 minutes.
3. Place in the air fryer basket and sprinkle with sesame seeds.
4. Cook for 10 minutes, garnishing with green onions before serving.

7. Coconut Shrimp

 Yield:
2 servings

 Prep time:
10 minutes

 Cook time:
12 minutes

 Cooking Temperature:
400°F (200°C)

 Cooking Method:
Fry

Ingredients:
- 1 lb shrimp, peeled and deveined
- 1/2 cup shredded coconut
- 1/2 cup breadcrumbs
- 1 egg, beaten
- Salt and pepper to taste

Directions:
1. Preheat the air fryer to 400°F (200°C).
2. Dip shrimp in beaten egg, then coat with a mixture of shredded coconut and breadcrumbs.
3. Place shrimp in the air fryer basket.
4. Cook for 12 minutes, flipping halfway through.

Nutritional Information

250 calories, 20g protein, 18g carbohydrates, 10g fat, 2g fiber, 200mg cholesterol, 350mg sodium, 280mg potassium.

8. Lemon Butter Tilapia

 Yield:
2 servings

 Prep time:
5 minutes

 Cook time:
10 minutes

 Cooking Temperature:
375°F (190°C)

 Cooking Method:
Fry

Ingredients:
- 2 tilapia fillets
- 2 tablespoons butter, melted
- Juice of 1 lemon
- Salt and pepper to taste

Directions:
1. Preheat the air fryer to 375°F (190°C).
2. Brush tilapia fillets with melted butter, lemon juice, salt, and pepper.
3. Place in the air fryer basket.
4. Cook for 10 minutes.

Nutritional Information

220 calories, 25g protein, 1g carbohydrates, 12g fat, 0g fiber, 70mg cholesterol, 50mg sodium, 300mg potassium.

9. Mahi-Mahi with Pineapple Salsa

 Yield:
2 servings

 Prep time:
10 minutes

 Cook time:
12 minutes

 Cooking Temperature:
400°F (200°C)

 Cooking Method:
Fry

Ingredients:
- 2 mahi-mahi fillets
- 1 tablespoon olive oil
- Salt and pepper to taste
- 1 cup fresh pineapple, diced
- 1/4 cup red onion, diced
- 1 tablespoon cilantro, chopped

Nutritional Information

250 calories, 28g protein, 10g carbohydrates, 10g fat, 1g fiber, 70mg cholesterol, 90mg sodium, 400mg potassium.

Directions:
1. Preheat the air fryer to 400°F (200°C).
2. Brush mahi-mahi fillets with olive oil, and season with salt and pepper.
3. Place fillets in the air fryer basket and cook for 12 minutes.
4. Meanwhile, mix pineapple, red onion, and cilantro in a bowl. Serve salsa on top of the cooked mahi-mahi.

10. Crab Cakes

 Yield:
2 servings

 Prep time:
10 minutes

 Cook time:
12 minutes

 Cooking Temperature:
375°F (190°C)

 Cooking Method:
Fry

Ingredients:
- 1 cup lump crab meat
- 1/4 cup breadcrumbs
- 1 egg, beaten
- 1 tablespoon Dijon mustard
- Salt and pepper to taste

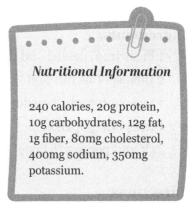

Nutritional Information

240 calories, 20g protein, 10g carbohydrates, 12g fat, 1g fiber, 80mg cholesterol, 400mg sodium, 350mg potassium.

Directions:
1. Preheat the air fryer to 375°F (190°C).
2. In a bowl, mix crab meat, breadcrumbs, egg, Dijon mustard, salt, and pepper.
3. Form the mixture into patties and place in the air fryer basket.
4. Cook for 12 minutes, flipping halfway.

11. Fish and Chips

 Yield:
2 servings

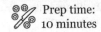 Prep time:
10 minutes

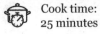 Cook time:
25 minutes

 Cooking Temperature:
400°F (200°C)

 Cooking Method:
Fry

Ingredients:

- 2 cod fillets
- 1 cup potato wedges
- 1 tablespoon olive oil
- Salt and pepper to taste
- 1 tablespoon malt vinegar (for serving)

Nutritional Information

350 calories, 25g protein, 40g carbohydrates, 10g fat, 4g fiber, 60mg cholesterol, 320mg sodium, 500mg potassium.

Directions:

1. Preheat the air fryer to 400°F (200°C).
2. Toss potato wedges with olive oil, salt, and pepper. Place in the air fryer basket.
3. Cook for 15 minutes, shaking halfway through. Add cod fillets and cook for an additional 10 minutes.
4. Serve with malt vinegar.

12. Grilled Shrimp

 Yield:
2 servings

 Prep time:
5 minutes

 Cook time:
10 minutes

 Cooking Temperature:
400°F (200°C)

 Cooking Method:
Fry

Ingredients:

- 1 lb shrimp, peeled and deveined
- 2 tablespoons olive oil
- 1 teaspoon garlic powder
- 1 teaspoon paprika
- Salt and pepper to taste

Nutritional Information

200 calories, 24g protein, 2g carbohydrates, 10g fat, 0g fiber, 150mg cholesterol, 320mg sodium, 300mg potassium.

Directions:

1. Preheat the air fryer to 400°F (200°C).
2. Toss shrimp with olive oil, garlic powder, paprika, salt, and pepper.
3. Place shrimp in the air fryer basket.
4. Cook for 10 minutes, shaking halfway through.

13. Baked Cod with Herbs

 Yield: 2 servings   Prep time: 5 minutes   Cook time: 12 minutes   Cooking Temperature: 375°F (190°C)   Cooking Method: Fry

Ingredients:

- 2 cod fillets
- 1 tablespoon olive oil
- 1 teaspoon mixed herbs (thyme, oregano, rosemary)
- Salt and pepper to taste

Directions:

1. Preheat the air fryer to 375°F (190°C).
2. Brush cod fillets with olive oil, and season with mixed herbs, salt, and pepper.
3. Place in the air fryer basket.
4. Cook for 12 minutes.

Nutritional Information

220 calories, 30g protein, 0g carbohydrates, 10g fat, 0g fiber, 75mg cholesterol, 60mg sodium, 400mg potassium.

14. Seafood Paella

 Yield: 2 servings   Prep time: 10 minutes   Cook time: 20 minutes   Cooking Temperature: 360°F (180°C)   Cooking Method: Bake

Ingredients:

- 1 cup cooked rice
- 1/2 cup shrimp, peeled and deveined
- 1/2 cup mussels (cleaned)
- 1/4 cup peas
- 1 teaspoon saffron or turmeric
- Salt and pepper to taste

Nutritional Information

350 calories, 25g protein, 40g carbohydrates, 8g fat, 3g fiber, 70mg cholesterol, 600mg sodium, 450mg potassium.

Directions:

1. Preheat the air fryer to 360°F (180°C).
2. In a bowl, mix cooked rice, shrimp, mussels, peas, saffron/turmeric, salt, and pepper.
3. Pour the mixture into a small baking dish that fits in the air fryer.
4. Cook for 20 minutes until heated through.

15. Lemon Pepper Fish

 Yield:
2 servings

 Prep time:
5 minutes

 Cook time:
12 minutes

 Cooking Temperature:
400°F (200°C)

 Cooking Method:
Fry

Ingredients:

- 2 fish fillets (such as tilapia or cod)
- 1 tablespoon olive oil
- 1 tablespoon lemon pepper seasoning
- Salt to taste

Nutritional Information

200 calories, 25g protein, 0g carbohydrates, 10g fat, 0g fiber, 60mg cholesterol, 60mg sodium, 300mg potassium.

Directions:

1. Preheat the air fryer to 400°F (200°C).
2. Brush fish fillets with olive oil and season with lemon pepper and salt.
3. Place in the air fryer basket.
4. Cook for 12 minutes.

16. Coconut Curry Fish

 Yield:
2 servings

 Prep time:
10 minutes

 Cook time:
15 minutes

 Cooking Temperature:
375°F (190°C)

 Cooking Method:
Fry

Ingredients:

- 2 fish fillets (such as salmon or tilapia)
- 1/4 cup coconut milk
- 1 tablespoon curry powder
- Salt to taste

Nutritional Information

250 calories, 30g protein, 5g carbohydrates, 12g fat, 0g fiber, 60mg cholesterol, 150mg sodium, 400mg potassium.

Directions:

1. Preheat the air fryer to 375°F (190°C).
2. In a bowl, mix coconut milk, curry powder, and salt. Coat the fish fillets in the mixture.
3. Place fish in the air fryer basket.
4. Cook for 15 minutes.

17. Fish Sticks

 Yield:
2 servings

 Prep time:
10 minutes

 Cook time:
10 minutes

 Cooking Temperature:
400°F (200°C)

 Cooking Method:
Fry

Ingredients:

- 1 lb white fish fillets, cut into strips
- 1/2 cup breadcrumbs
- 1 egg, beaten
- 1/4 cup flour
- Salt and pepper to taste

Nutritional Information

230 calories, 20g protein, 25g carbohydrates, 8g fat, 1g fiber, 60mg cholesterol, 300mg sodium, 300mg potassium.

Directions:

1. Preheat the air fryer to 400°F (200°C).
2. Dip fish strips in flour, then egg, and coat with breadcrumbs mixed with salt and pepper.
3. Place in the air fryer basket.
4. Cook for 10 minutes, flipping halfway.

18. Clams Casino

 Yield:
2 servings

 Prep time:
10 minutes

 Cook time:
12 minutes

 Cooking Temperature:
350°F (175°C)

 Cooking Method:
Bake

Ingredients:

- 12 clams, shucked
- 1/2 cup breadcrumbs
- 1/4 cup bell pepper, diced
- 2 tablespoons parsley, chopped
- 1 tablespoon olive oil
- Salt and pepper to taste

Nutritional Information

200 calories, 8g protein, 30g carbohydrates, 6g fat, 2g fiber, 25mg cholesterol, 300mg sodium, 250mg potassium.

Directions:

1. Preheat the air fryer to 350°F (175°C).
2. In a bowl, mix breadcrumbs, bell pepper, parsley, olive oil, salt, and pepper.
3. Spoon the mixture onto each clam.
4. Place clams in the air fryer and cook for 12 minutes.

19. Lemon Dill Shrimp

 Yield:
2 servings Prep time:
5 minutes   Cook time:
8 minutes Cooking Temperature:
400°F (200°C) Cooking Method:
Fry

Ingredients:

- 1 lb shrimp, peeled and deveined
- 1 tablespoon olive oil
- Juice of 1 lemon
- 1 teaspoon dried dill
- Salt and pepper to taste

Nutritional Information

180 calories, 24g protein, 2g carbohydrates, 8g fat, 0g fiber, 200mg cholesterol, 300mg sodium, 250mg potassium.

Directions:

1. Preheat the air fryer to 400°F (200°C).
2. Toss shrimp with olive oil, lemon juice, dill, salt, and pepper.
3. Place shrimp in the air fryer basket.
4. Cook for 8 minutes, shaking halfway through.

20. Fish Curry

 Yield:
2 servings Prep time:
10 minutes   Cook time:
15 minutes Cooking Temperature:
375°F (190°C) Cooking Method:
Fry

Ingredients:

- 2 fish fillets (such as cod or tilapia)
- 1/2 cup coconut milk
- 1 tablespoon curry powder
- 1 teaspoon ginger, minced
- Salt to taste

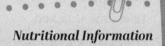

Nutritional Information

250 calories, 30g protein, 8g carbohydrates, 12g fat, 0g fiber, 75mg cholesterol, 150mg sodium, 400mg potassium.

Directions:

1. Preheat the air fryer to 375°F (190° C).
2. In a bowl, mix coconut milk, curry powder, ginger, and salt. Coat the fish fillets in the mixture.
3. Place fish in the air fryer basket.
4. Cook for 15 minutes.

Chapter 7

Poultry Favourites

1. Lemon Herb Chicken Thighs

 Yield:
4 servings

 Prep time:
5 minutes

 Cook time:
25 minutes

 Cooking Temperature:
400°F (200°C)

 Cooking Method:
Fry

Ingredients:

- 4 chicken thighs (boneless, skinless)
- 1 tablespoon olive oil
- Juice of 1 lemon
- 1 teaspoon dried oregano
- Salt and pepper to taste

Nutritional Information

230 calories, 25g protein, 0g carbohydrates, 14g fat, 0g fiber, 85mg cholesterol, 230mg sodium, 400mg potassium.

Directions:

1. Preheat the air fryer to 400°F (200°C).
2. In a bowl, mix olive oil, lemon juice, oregano, salt, and pepper. Coat chicken thighs in the mixture.
3. Place the chicken in the air fryer basket.
4. Cook for 25 minutes, flipping halfway through.

2. BBQ Chicken Drumsticks

 Yield:
4 servings

 Prep time:
5 minutes

 Cook time:
25 minutes

 Cooking Temperature:
400°F (200°C)

 Cooking Method:
Fry

Ingredients:

- 8 chicken drumsticks
- 1/4 cup BBQ sauce
- Salt and pepper to taste

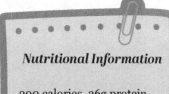

Nutritional Information

290 calories, 26g protein, 10g carbohydrates, 18g fat, 0g fiber, 90mg cholesterol, 400mg sodium, 500mg potassium.

Directions:

1. Preheat the air fryer to 400°F (200°C).
2. Season drumsticks with salt and pepper, then brush with BBQ sauce.
3. Place in the air fryer basket.
4. Cook for 25 minutes, turning halfway and basting with more BBQ sauce if desired.

3. Herb-Roasted Chicken Breasts

 Yield:
2 servings

 Prep time:
5 minutes

 Cook time:
20 minutes

 Cooking Temperature:
380°F (190°C)

 Cooking Method:
Roast

Ingredients:

- 2 boneless, skinless chicken breasts
- 1 tablespoon olive oil
- 1 teaspoon dried thyme
- Salt and pepper to taste

Nutritional Information

240 calories, 32g protein, 0g carbohydrates, 11g fat, 0g fiber, 70mg cholesterol, 60mg sodium, 400mg potassium.

Directions:

1. Preheat the air fryer to 380°F (190°C).
2. Rub chicken breasts with olive oil, thyme, salt, and pepper.
3. Place in the air fryer basket.
4. Cook for 20 minutes, flipping halfway through.

4. Honey Garlic Chicken Thighs

 Yield:
4 servings

 Prep time:
5 minutes

 Cook time:
25 minutes

 Cooking Temperature:
400°F (200°C)

 Cooking Method:
Fry

Ingredients:

- 4 chicken thighs (bone-in, skin-on)
- 1/4 cup honey
- 2 tablespoons soy sauce
- 3 cloves garlic, minced
- Salt and pepper to taste

Nutritional Information

280 calories, 25g protein, 26g carbohydrates, 10g fat, 0g fiber, 90mg cholesterol, 300mg sodium, 400mg potassium.

Directions:

1. Preheat the air fryer to 400°F (200°C).
2. In a bowl, mix honey, soy sauce, garlic, salt, and pepper. Coat chicken thighs in the mixture.
3. Place the chicken in the air fryer basket.
4. Cook for 25 minutes, flipping halfway.

5. Chicken Fajitas

 Yield:
4 servings

 Prep time:
10 minutes

 Cook time:
15 minutes

 Cooking Temperature:
400°F (200°C)

 Cooking Method:
Fry

Ingredients:

- 1 lb boneless, skinless chicken breasts, sliced
- 1 bell pepper, sliced
- 1 onion, sliced
- 2 tablespoons fajita seasoning
- 1 tablespoon olive oil

Nutritional Information

240 calories, 34g protein, 8g carbohydrates, 7g fat, 2g fiber, 70mg cholesterol, 350mg sodium, 400mg potassium.

Directions:

1. Preheat the air fryer to 400°F (200°C).
2. In a bowl, toss the chicken, bell pepper, onion, fajita seasoning, and olive oil.
3. Place the mixture in the air fryer basket.
4. Cook for 15 minutes, shaking the basket halfway through.

6. Greek Chicken Kebabs

 Yield:
4 servings

 Prep time:
10 minutes

 Cook time:
15 minutes

 Cooking Temperature:
400°F (200°C)

 Cooking Method:
Fry

Ingredients:

- 1 lb chicken breast, cubed
- 1/4 cup olive oil
- 2 tablespoons lemon juice
- 1 tablespoon oregano
- Salt and pepper to taste
- Skewers

Nutritional Information

260 calories, 30g protein, 0g carbohydrates, 14g fat, 0g fiber, 80mg cholesterol, 80mg sodium, 350mg potassium.

Directions:

1. Preheat the air fryer to 400°F (200°C).
2. In a bowl, mix olive oil, lemon juice, oregano, salt, and pepper. Toss chicken in the marinade.
3. Thread chicken onto skewers.
4. Place skewers in the air fryer basket and cook for 15 minutes, turning halfway.

7. Chicken Parmesan

 Yield:
2 servings

 Prep time:
10 minutes

 Cook time:
15 minutes

 Cooking Temperature:
375°F (190°C)

 Cooking Method:
Fry

Ingredients:
- 2 chicken breasts
- 1/2 cup breadcrumbs
- 1/4 cup grated Parmesan cheese
- 1/2 cup marinara sauce
- 1/2 cup shredded mozzarella cheese

Nutritional Information

350 calories, 40g protein, 16g carbohydrates, 15g fat, 1g fiber, 90mg cholesterol, 600mg sodium, 400mg potassium.

Directions:
1. Preheat the air fryer to 375°F (190°C).
2. In a bowl, mix breadcrumbs and Parmesan cheese. Coat chicken breasts in the mixture.
3. Place chicken in the air fryer basket and cook for 10 minutes.
4. Top with marinara and mozzarella, then cook for an additional 5 minutes.

8. Chicken and Broccoli

 Yield:
2 servings

 Prep time:
10 minutes

 Cook time:
15 minutes

 Cooking Temperature:
400°F (200°C)

 Cooking Method:
Fry

Ingredients:
- 1 lb chicken breast, cubed
- 2 cups broccoli florets
- 2 tablespoons soy sauce
- 1 tablespoon olive oil
- Salt and pepper to taste

Nutritional Information

300 calories, 35g protein, 8g carbohydrates, 10g fat, 4g fiber, 75mg cholesterol, 400mg sodium, 500mg potassium.

Directions:
1. Preheat the air fryer to 400°F (200°C).
2. In a bowl, toss chicken and broccoli with soy sauce, olive oil, salt, and pepper.
3. Place in the air fryer basket.
4. Cook for 15 minutes, shaking halfway through.

9. Chicken Satay

 Yield:
2 servings

 Prep time:
10 minutes

 Cook time:
12 minutes

 Cooking Temperature:
400°F (200°C)

 Cooking Method:
Fry

Ingredients:

- 1 lb chicken breast, cut into strips
- 1/4 cup peanut butter
- 2 tablespoons soy sauce
- 1 tablespoon lime juice
- 1 teaspoon curry powder

Directions:

1. Preheat the air fryer to 400°F (200°C).
2. In a bowl, mix peanut butter, soy sauce, lime juice, and curry powder. Toss chicken strips in the mixture.
3. Place chicken in the air fryer basket.
4. Cook for 12 minutes, turning halfway.

Nutritional Information

320 calories, 32g protein, 8g carbohydrates, 18g fat, 1g fiber, 70mg cholesterol, 300mg sodium, 400mg potassium.

10. Chicken Lettuce Wraps

 Yield:
2 servings

 Prep time:
5 minutes

 Cook time:
10 minutes

 Cooking Temperature:
380°F (190°C)

 Cooking Method:
Fry

Ingredients:

- 1 lb ground chicken
- 1/4 cup soy sauce
- 1 tablespoon hoisin sauce
- 1 teaspoon ginger, minced
- Butter lettuce leaves for wrapping

Directions:

1. Preheat the air fryer to 380°F (190°C).
2. In a bowl, mix ground chicken, soy sauce, hoisin sauce, and ginger.
3. Place the mixture in the air fryer basket.
4. Cook for 10 minutes, breaking up the chicken halfway through. Serve in lettuce leaves.

Nutritional Information

240 calories, 30g protein, 6g carbohydrates, 10g fat, 1g fiber, 80mg cholesterol, 400mg sodium, 300mg potassium.

11. Orange Chicken

 Yield:
2 servings

 Prep time:
5 minutes

 Cook time:
15 minutes

Cooking Temperature:
400°F (200°C)

 Cooking Method:
Fry

Ingredients:

- 1 lb chicken breast, cubed
- 1/4 cup orange juice
- 2 tablespoons soy sauce
- 1 tablespoon honey
- Salt and pepper to taste

Nutritional Information

260 calories, 28g protein, 14g carbohydrates, 8g fat, 0g fiber, 75mg cholesterol, 350mg sodium, 400mg potassium.

Directions:

1. Preheat the air fryer to 400°F (200°C).
2. In a bowl, mix orange juice, soy sauce, honey, salt, and pepper. Toss chicken in the mixture.
3. Place chicken in the air fryer basket.
4. Cook for 15 minutes, shaking halfway through.

12. Chicken Quesadillas

 Yield:
2 servings

 Prep time:
10 minutes

 Cook time:
10 minutes

 Cooking Temperature:
380°F (190°C)

 Cooking Method:
Fry

Ingredients:

- 2 whole wheat tortillas
- 1 cup cooked chicken, shredded
- 1/2 cup shredded cheese (cheddar or mozzarella)
- 1/4 cup salsa

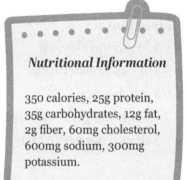

Nutritional Information

350 calories, 25g protein, 35g carbohydrates, 12g fat, 2g fiber, 60mg cholesterol, 600mg sodium, 300mg potassium.

Directions:

1. Preheat the air fryer to 380°F (190°C).
2. Place one tortilla in the air fryer basket. Top with chicken, cheese, and salsa, then place the second tortilla on top.
3. Cook for 10 minutes, flipping halfway through.

13. Pesto Chicken Breasts

 Yield:
2 servings

 Prep time:
5 minutes

 Cook time:
20 minutes

 Cooking Temperature:
375°F (190°C)

 Cooking Method:
Fry

Ingredients:
- 2 boneless, skinless chicken breasts
- 1/4 cup pesto
- Salt and pepper to taste

Directions:
1. Preheat the air fryer to 375°F (190°C).
2. Spread pesto over chicken breasts and season with salt and pepper.
3. Place in the air fryer basket.
4. Cook for 20 minutes, flipping halfway.

Nutritional Information

280 calories, 35g protein, 4g carbohydrates, 14g fat, 1g fiber, 70mg cholesterol, 300mg sodium, 450mg potassium.

14. Chicken Fritters

 Yield:
2 servings

 Prep time:
10 minutes

 Cook time:
12 minutes

 Cooking Temperature:
400°F (200°C)

 Cooking Method:
Fry

Ingredients:
- 1 lb ground chicken
- 1/4 cup breadcrumbs
- 1 egg, beaten
- 1 teaspoon garlic powder
- Salt and pepper to taste

Directions:
1. Preheat the air fryer to 400°F (200°C).
2. In a bowl, mix ground chicken, breadcrumbs, egg, garlic powder, salt, and pepper.
3. Form the mixture into patties and place in the air fryer basket.
4. Cook for 12 minutes, flipping halfway.

Nutritional Information

240 calories, 28g protein, 10g carbohydrates, 8g fat, 0g fiber, 100mg cholesterol, 300mg sodium, 280mg potassium.

15. Chicken Cacciatore

 Yield:
2 servings

 Prep time:
10 minutes

 Cook time:
25 minutes

 Cooking Temperature:
375°F (190°C)

 Cooking Method:
Bake

Ingredients:

- 2 chicken thighs, bone-in
- 1/2 cup marinara sauce
- 1/2 cup bell peppers, sliced
- 1/4 cup onions, sliced
- 1 teaspoon Italian seasoning

Nutritional Information

320 calories, 30g protein, 10g carbohydrates, 18g fat, 2g fiber, 85mg cholesterol, 400mg sodium, 350mg potassium.

Directions:

1. Preheat the air fryer to 375°F (190°C).
2. Place chicken thighs in the air fryer basket and cover with marinara sauce, bell peppers, onions, and Italian seasoning.
3. Cook for 25 minutes, flipping halfway through.

16. Chicken Stir-Fry

 Yield:
2 servings

 Prep time:
10 minutes

 Cook time:
15 minutes

 Cooking Temperature:
400°F (200°C)

 Cooking Method:
Fry

Ingredients:

- 1 lb chicken breast, sliced
- 2 cups mixed vegetables (broccoli, bell peppers, snap peas)
- 2 tablespoons soy sauce
- 1 tablespoon olive oil

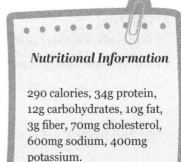

Nutritional Information

290 calories, 34g protein, 12g carbohydrates, 10g fat, 3g fiber, 70mg cholesterol, 600mg sodium, 400mg potassium.

Directions:

1. Preheat the air fryer to 400°F (200°C).
2. In a bowl, toss chicken and mixed vegetables with soy sauce and olive oil.
3. Place in the air fryer basket.
4. Cook for 15 minutes, shaking halfway through.

17. Chicken Shawarma

 Yield: 2 servings

 Prep time: 5 minutes

 Cook time: 15 minutes

 Cooking Temperature: 400°F (200°C)

 Cooking Method: Fry

Ingredients:
- 1 lb chicken thighs, boneless
- 2 tablespoons olive oil
- 1 tablespoon shawarma spice blend
- Salt and pepper to taste

Nutritional Information

320 calories, 30g protein, 4g carbohydrates, 20g fat, 0g fiber, 80mg cholesterol, 350mg sodium, 400mg potassium.

Directions:
1. Preheat the air fryer to 400°F (200°C).
2. Rub chicken thighs with olive oil, shawarma spice blend, salt, and pepper.
3. Place in the air fryer basket.
4. Cook for 15 minutes, flipping halfway.

18. Chicken and Rice

 Yield: 2 servings

 Prep time: 10 minutes

 Cook time: 20 minutes

 Cooking Temperature: 360°F (180°C)

 Cooking Method: Bake

Ingredients:
- 2 boneless, skinless chicken breasts
- 1 cup cooked rice (brown or white)
- 1/2 cup chicken broth
- 1 cup broccoli florets
- Salt and pepper to taste

Nutritional Information

380 calories, 35g protein, 50g carbohydrates, 6g fat, 3g fiber, 70mg cholesterol, 400mg sodium, 450mg potassium.

Directions:
1. Preheat the air fryer to 360°F (180°C).
2. In a bowl, mix cooked rice, chicken broth, broccoli, salt, and pepper.
3. Place the mixture in a small baking dish that fits in the air fryer. Top with chicken breasts.
4. Cook for 20 minutes until chicken is cooked through.

19. Chicken Caesar Wraps

 Yield:
2 servings
 Prep time:
10 minutes
 Cook time:
10 minutes
 Cooking Temperature:
380°F (190°C)
 Cooking Method:
Fry

Ingredients:

- 1 lb cooked chicken, shredded
- 1/4 cup Caesar dressing
- 2 large lettuce leaves
- 2 whole wheat tortillas
- 1/4 cup grated Parmesan cheese

Nutritional Information

300 calories, 30g protein, 20g carbohydrates, 12g fat, 2g fiber, 45mg cholesterol, 600mg sodium, 350mg potassium.

Directions:

1. Preheat the air fryer to 380°F (190°C).
2. In a bowl, mix shredded chicken with Caesar dressing and Parmesan cheese.
3. Fill tortillas with the mixture and wrap tightly.
4. Place in the air fryer and cook for 10 minutes.

20. Chicken Taquitos

 Yield:
2 servings
 Prep time:
10 minutes
 Cook time:
12 minutes
 Cooking Temperature:
400°F (200°C)
 Cooking Method:
Fry

Ingredients:

- 1 lb shredded cooked chicken
- 1/2 cup cheese (cheddar or Mexican blend)
- 4 small corn tortillas
- 1 tablespoon taco seasoning

Nutritional Information

350 calories, 28g protein, 30g carbohydrates, 12g fat, 2g fiber, 70mg cholesterol, 400mg sodium, 400mg potassium.

Directions:

1. Preheat the air fryer to 400°F (200°C).
2. In a bowl, mix shredded chicken, cheese, and taco seasoning.
3. Spoon the mixture onto corn tortillas and roll tightly
4. Place taquitos in the air fryer basket and cook for 12 minutes.

Chapter 8

Beef, Pork and Lamb

1. Lemon Garlic Beef Skewers

 Yield:
4 servings

 Prep time:
10 minutes

 Cook time:
12 minutes

 Cooking Temperature:
400°F (200°C)

 Cooking Method:
Fry

Ingredients:

- 1 lb beef sirloin, cut into cubes
- 2 tablespoons olive oil
- Juice of 1 lemon
- 2 cloves garlic, minced
- Salt and pepper to taste
- Skewers

Nutritional Information

250 calories, 32g protein,
0g carbohydrates, 12g fat,
0g fiber, 85mg cholesterol,
60mg sodium, 400mg
potassium.

Directions:

1. Preheat the air fryer to 400°F (200°C).
2. In a bowl, mix olive oil, lemon juice, garlic, salt, and pepper. Toss beef cubes in the mixture.
3. Thread beef onto skewers.
4. Place skewers in the air fryer and cook for 12 minutes, turning halfway.

2. BBQ Pork Chops

 Yield:
2 servings

 Prep time:
5 minutes

 Cook time:
12 minutes

 Cooking Temperature:
400°F (200°C)

 Cooking Method:
Fry

Ingredients:

- 2 boneless pork chops
- 2 tablespoons BBQ sauce
- Salt and pepper to taste

Nutritional Information

220 calories, 26g protein,
8g carbohydrates, 10g fat,
0g fiber, 70mg cholesterol,
300mg sodium, 350mg
potassium.

Directions:

1. Preheat the air fryer to 400°F (200°C).
2. Season pork chops with salt and pepper, then brush with BBQ sauce.
3. Place in the air fryer basket.
4. Cook for 12 minutes, flipping halfway.

3. Herb-Crusted Lamb Chops

 Yield:
2 servings   Prep time:
5 minutes   Cook time:
15 minutes   Cooking Temperature:
375°F (190°C)   Cooking Method:
Fry

Ingredients:

- 4 lamb chops
- 1 tablespoon olive oil
- 1 teaspoon rosemary
- 1 teaspoon thyme
- Salt and pepper to taste

Nutritional Information

320 calories, 28g protein, 0g carbohydrates, 22g fat, 0g fiber, 80mg cholesterol, 70mg sodium, 400mg potassium.

Directions:

1. Preheat the air fryer to 375°F (190°C).
2. Rub lamb chops with olive oil, rosemary, thyme, salt, and pepper.
3. Place in the air fryer basket.
4. Cook for 15 minutes, flipping halfway.

4. Beef Meatballs

 Yield:
4 servings   Prep time:
10 minutes   Cook time:
15 minutes   Cooking Temperature:
400°F (200°C)   Cooking Method:
Fry

Ingredients:

- 1 lb ground beef
- 1/2 cup breadcrumbs
- 1/4 cup grated Parmesan cheese
- 1 egg
- 1 teaspoon Italian seasoning
- Salt and pepper to taste

Nutritional Information

280 calories, 26g protein, 10g carbohydrates, 15g fat, 0g fiber, 70mg cholesterol, 450mg sodium, 300mg potassium.

Directions:

1. Preheat the air fryer to 400°F (200°C).
2. In a bowl, mix ground beef, breadcrumbs, Parmesan, egg, Italian seasoning, salt, and pepper.
3. Form into meatballs and place in the air fryer basket.
4. Cook for 15 minutes, shaking halfway.

5. Beef Tacos

 Yield: 2 servings   Prep time: 10 minutes   Cook time: 8 minutes   Cooking Temperature: 400°F (200°C)   Cooking Method: Fry

Ingredients:

- 1 lb ground beef
- 1 tablespoon taco seasoning
- 4 small corn tortillas
- Optional toppings: lettuce, tomato, cheese

Directions:

1. Preheat the air fryer to 400°F (200°C).
2. In a bowl, mix ground beef with taco seasoning.
3. Form beef into small patties and place in the air fryer basket.
4. Cook for 8 minutes, then serve in corn tortillas with toppings.

Nutritional Information

320 calories, 26g protein, 12g carbohydrates, 18g fat, 4g fiber, 60mg cholesterol, 400mg sodium, 350mg potassium.

6. Spicy Sausage & Peppers

 Yield: 2 servings   Prep time: 5 minutes   Cook time: 15 minutes   Cooking Temperature: 400°F (200°C)   Cooking Method: Fry

Ingredients:

- 2 spicy sausage links, sliced
- 1 bell pepper, sliced
- 1 onion, sliced
- 1 tablespoon olive oil
- Salt and pepper to taste

Directions:

1. Preheat the air fryer to 400°F (200°C).
2. Toss sausage, bell pepper, onion, olive oil, salt, and pepper in a bowl.
3. Place in the air fryer basket.
4. Cook for 15 minutes, shaking halfway.

Nutritional Information

350 calories, 20g protein, 10g carbohydrates, 25g fat, 2g fiber, 80mg cholesterol, 600mg sodium, 400mg potassium.

7. Maple Glazed Pork Chops

 Yield:
2 servings
 Prep time:
5 minutes
 Cook time:
12 minutes
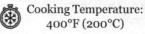 Cooking Temperature:
400°F (200°C)
 Cooking Method:
Fry

Ingredients:
- 2 boneless pork chops
- 2 tablespoons maple syrup
- Salt and pepper to taste

Directions:
1. Preheat the air fryer to 400°F (200°C).
2. Season pork chops with salt and pepper, then brush with maple syrup.
3. Place in the air fryer basket.
4. Cook for 12 minutes, flipping halfway.

Nutritional Information

270 calories, 25g protein, 12g carbohydrates, 14g fat, 0g fiber, 70mg cholesterol, 60mg sodium, 300mg potassium.

8. Beef and Broccoli

 Yield:
2 servings
 Prep time:
10 minutes
 Cook time:
15 minutes
 Cooking Temperature:
380°F (190°C)
 Cooking Method:
Fry

Ingredients:
- 1 lb beef sirloin, sliced thin
- 2 cups broccoli florets
- 2 tablespoons soy sauce
- 1 tablespoon olive oil
- 1 teaspoon garlic powder

Directions:
1. Preheat the air fryer to 380°F (190°C).
2. In a bowl, toss beef, broccoli, soy sauce, olive oil, and garlic powder.
3. Place in the air fryer basket.
4. Cook for 15 minutes, shaking halfway.

Nutritional Information

300 calories, 35g protein, 10g carbohydrates, 12g fat, 4g fiber, 70mg cholesterol, 400mg sodium, 350mg potassium.

9. Beef Stroganoff

 Yield:
4 servings

 Prep time:
10 minutes

 Cook time:
15 minutes

 Cooking Temperature:
360°F (180°C)

 Cooking Method:
Bake

Ingredients:
- 1 lb beef strips
- 1 cup mushrooms, sliced
- 1/2 cup beef broth
- 1/4 cup sour cream
- Salt and pepper to taste

Directions:
1. Preheat the air fryer to 360°F (180°C).
2. In a bowl, mix beef, mushrooms, beef broth, salt, and pepper.
3. Place in a small baking dish that fits in the air fryer.
4. Cook for 15 minutes, then stir in sour cream before serving.

Nutritional Information

320 calories, 30g protein, 8g carbohydrates, 20g fat, 1g fiber, 75mg cholesterol, 400mg sodium, 300mg potassium.

10. Beef Enchiladas

 Yield:
2 servings

 Prep time:
10 minutes

 Cook time:
15 minutes

 Cooking Temperature:
375°F (190°C)

 Cooking Method:
Bake

Ingredients:
- 1 lb ground beef
- 4 corn tortillas
- 1 cup enchilada sauce
- 1/2 cup shredded cheese (cheddar or Mexican blend)

Directions:
1. Preheat the air fryer to 375°F (190°C).
2. Cook ground beef in a skillet until browned, then fill tortillas with beef and roll.
3. Place enchiladas in the air fryer basket and top with enchilada sauce and cheese.
4. Cook for 15 minutes.

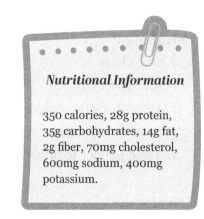

Nutritional Information

350 calories, 28g protein, 35g carbohydrates, 14g fat, 2g fiber, 70mg cholesterol, 600mg sodium, 400mg potassium.

11. Pork Tenderloin with Apples

 Yield:
2 servings

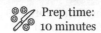 Prep time:
10 minutes

 Cook time:
12 minutes

 Cooking Temperature:
375°F (190°C)

 Cooking Method:
Fry

Ingredients:
- 1 lb pork tenderloin
- 1 apple, sliced
- 1 tablespoon olive oil
- 1 teaspoon cinnamon
- Salt and pepper to taste

Nutritional Information

280 calories, 30g protein, 15g carbohydrates, 10g fat, 2g fiber, 70mg cholesterol, 80mg sodium, 300mg potassium.

Directions:
1. Preheat the air fryer to 375°F (190°C).
2. Rub pork tenderloin with olive oil, cinnamon, salt, and pepper.
3. Place pork in the air fryer basket and surround it with apple slices.
4. Cook for 20 minutes, flipping halfway.

12. Lamb Chops

 Yield:
2 servings

 Prep time:
5 minutes

 Cook time:
12 minutes

 Cooking Temperature:
400°F (200°C)

 Cooking Method:
Fry

Ingredients:
- 4 lamb chops
- 1 tablespoon olive oil
- 1 teaspoon garlic powder
- 1 teaspoon rosemary
- Salt and pepper to taste

Nutritional Information

320 calories, 28g protein, 0g carbohydrates, 22g fat, 0g fiber, 80mg cholesterol, 70mg sodium, 400mg potassium.

Directions:
1. Preheat the air fryer to 400°F (200°C).
2. Rub lamb chops with olive oil, garlic powder, rosemary, salt, and pepper.
3. Place in the air fryer basket.
4. Cook for 12 minutes, flipping halfway.

13. Pork Belly Bites

 Yield:
2 servings

 Prep time:
10 minutes

 Cook time:
15 minutes

 Cooking Temperature:
400°F (200°C)

 Cooking Method:
Fry

Ingredients:

- 1 lb pork belly, cut into bite-sized pieces
- 1 tablespoon soy sauce
- 1 tablespoon honey
- Salt and pepper to taste

Directions:

1. Preheat the air fryer to 400°F (200°C).
2. In a bowl, toss pork belly with soy sauce, honey, salt, and pepper.
3. Place in the air fryer basket.
4. Cook for 15 minutes, shaking halfway.

Nutritional Information

450 calories, 25g protein, 10g carbohydrates, 35g fat, 0g fiber, 100mg cholesterol, 500mg sodium, 300mg potassium.

14. Beef Burgers

 Yield:
2 servings

 Prep time:
5 minutes

 Cook time:
10 minutes

 Cooking Temperature:
375°F (190°C)

 Cooking Method:
Fry

Ingredients:

- 1 lb ground beef
- 1 teaspoon garlic powder
- 1 teaspoon onion powder
- Salt and pepper to taste

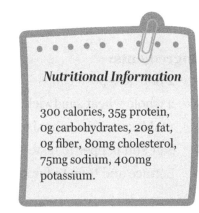

Nutritional Information

300 calories, 35g protein, 0g carbohydrates, 20g fat, 0g fiber, 80mg cholesterol, 75mg sodium, 400mg potassium.

Directions:

1. Preheat the air fryer to 375°F (190°C).
2. In a bowl, mix ground beef with garlic powder, onion powder, salt, and pepper.
3. Form into two patties and place in the air fryer basket.
4. Cook for 10 minutes, flipping halfway.

15. Lamb Kofta Kebabs

 Yield:
4 servings

 Prep time:
10 minutes

 Cook time:
15 minutes

 Cooking Temperature:
400°F (200°C)

 Cooking Method:
Fry

Ingredients:

- 1 lb ground lamb
- 1 tablespoon cumin
- 1 tablespoon coriander
- 2 cloves garlic, minced
- Salt and pepper to taste
- Skewers

Nutritional Information

320 calories, 25g protein, 0g carbohydrates, 25g fat, 0g fiber, 70mg cholesterol, 75mg sodium, 350mg potassium.

Directions:

1. Preheat the air fryer to 400°F (200°C).
2. In a bowl, mix ground lamb, cumin, coriander, garlic, salt, and pepper.
3. Form mixture onto skewers.
4. Place skewers in the air fryer and cook for 15 minutes, turning halfway.

16. Pork Chop Sandwiches

 Yield:
2 servings

 Prep time:
10 minutes

 Cook time:
12 minutes

 Cooking Temperature:
400°F (200°C)

 Cooking Method:
Fry

Ingredients:

- 2 boneless pork chops
- 2 whole wheat sandwich buns
- 1 tablespoon mayonnaise
- Salt and pepper to taste
- Lettuce and tomato for serving

Nutritional Information

360 calories, 30g protein, 30g carbohydrates, 14g fat, 2g fiber, 80mg cholesterol, 400mg sodium, 300mg potassium.

Directions:

1. Preheat the air fryer to 400°F (200°C).
2. Season pork chops with salt and pepper and place in the air fryer basket.
3. Cook for 12 minutes, flipping halfway.
4. Serve on buns with mayonnaise, lettuce, and tomato.

17. Beef Brisket

 Yield:
4 servings

 Prep time:
10 minutes

 Cook time:
45 minutes

 Cooking Temperature:
350°F (175°C)

 Cooking Method:
Roast

Ingredients:
- 1 lb beef brisket
- 1 tablespoon olive oil
- 2 teaspoons smoked paprika
- Salt and pepper to taste

Directions:
1. Preheat the air fryer to 350°F (175°C).
2. Rub brisket with olive oil, smoked paprika, salt, and pepper.
3. Place in the air fryer basket.
4. Cook for 45 minutes, flipping halfway.

Nutritional Information

380 calories, 30g protein, 0g carbohydrates, 30g fat, 0g fiber, 85mg cholesterol, 70mg sodium, 400mg potassium.

18. Lamb Burgers

 Yield:
2 servings

 Prep time:
5 minutes

 Cook time:
10 minutes

 Cooking Temperature:
375°F (190°C)

 Cooking Method:
Fry

Ingredients:
- 1 lb ground lamb
- 1 teaspoon garlic powder
- 1 teaspoon onion powder
- Salt and pepper to taste

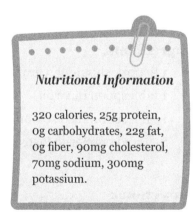

Nutritional Information

320 calories, 25g protein, 0g carbohydrates, 22g fat, 0g fiber, 90mg cholesterol, 70mg sodium, 300mg potassium.

Directions:
1. Preheat the air fryer to 375°F (190°C).
2. In a bowl, mix ground lamb with garlic powder, onion powder, salt, and pepper.
3. Form into two patties and place in the air fryer basket.
4. Cook for 10 minutes, flipping halfway.

19. Beef and Vegetable Skewers

 Yield:
4 servings

 Prep time:
10 minutes

 Cook time:
12 minutes

 Cooking Temperature:
400°F (200°C)

 Cooking Method:
Fry

Ingredients:

- 1 lb beef sirloin, cut into cubes
- 2 cups bell peppers, cut into chunks
- 1 onion, cut into chunks
- 2 tablespoons olive oil
- Salt and pepper to taste
- Skewers

Nutritional Information

290 calories, 32g protein,
10g carbohydrates, 12g fat,
3g fiber, 80mg cholesterol,
300mg sodium, 400mg
potassium.

Directions:

1. Preheat the air fryer to 400°F (200°C).
2. In a bowl, mix beef, bell peppers, onion, olive oil, salt, and pepper.
3. Thread beef and vegetables onto skewers.
4. Place skewers in the air fryer and cook for 12 minutes, turning halfway.

20. Pork Carnitas

 Yield:
4 servings

 Prep time:
10 minutes

 Cook time:
25 minutes

 Cooking Temperature:
400°F (200°C)

 Cooking Method:
Fry

Ingredients:

- 1 lb pork shoulder, cut into chunks
- 1 tablespoon olive oil
- 1 tablespoon taco seasoning
- Salt and pepper to taste

Nutritional Information

330 calories, 30g protein,
0g carbohydrates, 20g fat,
0g fiber, 80mg cholesterol,
70mg sodium, 400mg
potassium.

Directions:

1. Preheat the air fryer to 400°F (200°C).
2. Toss pork shoulder with olive oil, taco seasoning, salt, and pepper.
3. Place in the air fryer basket.
4. Cook for 25 minutes, shaking halfway through.

Chapter 9

Vegetarian Favourites

1. Stuffed Bell Peppers

 Yield: 4 servings   Prep time: 10 minutes   Cook time: 15 minutes   Cooking Temperature: 360°F (180°C)   Cooking Method: Bake

Ingredients:
- 4 bell peppers, halved and seeded
- 1 cup cooked quinoa
- 1 cup black beans, drained and rinsed
- 1/2 cup corn
- 1 teaspoon cumin
- 1/2 cup salsa

Nutritional Information

180 calories, 8g protein, 30g carbohydrates, 3g fat, 8g fiber, 0mg cholesterol, 230mg sodium, 300mg potassium.

Directions:
1. Preheat the air fryer to 360°F (180°C).
2. In a bowl, mix quinoa, black beans, corn, cumin, and salsa.
3. Stuff each bell pepper half with the mixture.
4. Place in the air fryer basket and cook for 15 minutes.

2. Zucchini Fries

 Yield: 4 servings   Prep time: 5 minutes   Cook time: 15 minutes   Cooking Temperature: 400°F (200°C)   Cooking Method: Fry

Ingredients:
- 2 medium zucchinis, cut into fries
- 1/2 cup breadcrumbs
- 1/4 cup grated Parmesan cheese
- 1 egg, beaten
- Salt and pepper to taste

Nutritional Information

150 calories, 6g protein, 20g carbohydrates, 7g fat, 2g fiber, 75mg cholesterol, 300mg sodium, 250mg potassium.

Directions:
1. Preheat the air fryer to 400°F (200°C).
2. Dip zucchini fries in beaten egg, then coat with a mixture of breadcrumbs, Parmesan, salt, and pepper.
3. Place in the air fryer basket.
4. Cook for 15 minutes, shaking halfway.

3. Eggplant Parmesan

 Yield:
4 servings

 Prep time:
10 minutes

 Cook time:
20 minutes

 Cooking Temperature:
375°F (190°C)

 Cooking Method:
Bake

Ingredients:

- 1 medium eggplant, sliced
- 1 cup marinara sauce
- 1 cup shredded mozzarella cheese
- 1/2 cup breadcrumbs
- 1 tablespoon olive oil
- Salt and pepper to taste

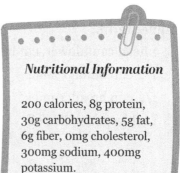

Nutritional Information

250 calories, 10g protein, 30g carbohydrates, 10g fat, 4g fiber, 30mg cholesterol, 500mg sodium, 350mg potassium.

Directions:

1. Preheat the air fryer to 375°F (190°C).
2. Brush eggplant slices with olive oil and season with salt and pepper. Dip in breadcrumbs.
3. Place in the air fryer basket and cook for 10 minutes.
4. Top with marinara sauce and mozzarella cheese, then cook for another 10 minutes.

4. Chickpea Fritters

 Yield:
4 servings

 Prep time:
10 minutes

 Cook time:
15 minutes

 Cooking Temperature:
375°F (190°C)

 Cooking Method:
Fry

Ingredients:

- 1 can (15 oz) chickpeas, drained and rinsed
- 1/4 cup breadcrumbs
- 1/4 cup onion, diced
- 1 tablespoon cumin
- Salt and pepper to taste

Nutritional Information

200 calories, 8g protein, 30g carbohydrates, 5g fat, 6g fiber, 0mg cholesterol, 300mg sodium, 400mg potassium.

Directions:

1. Preheat the air fryer to 375°F (190°C).
2. In a bowl, mash chickpeas and mix in breadcrumbs, onion, cumin, salt, and pepper.
3. Form mixture into small patties and place in the air fryer basket.
4. Cook for 15 minutes, flipping halfway.

5. Sweet Potato Wedges

 Yield: 4 servings   **Prep time:** 5 minutes   **Cook time:** 25 minutes   **Cooking Temperature:** 400°F (200°C)   **Cooking Method:** Fry

Ingredients:

- 2 large sweet potatoes, cut into wedges
- 2 tablespoons olive oil
- 1 teaspoon paprika
- Salt and pepper to taste

Directions:

1. Preheat the air fryer to 400°F (200°C).
2. Toss sweet potato wedges with olive oil, paprika, salt, and pepper.
3. Place in the air fryer basket.
4. Cook for 25 minutes, shaking halfway.

Nutritional Information

180 calories, 3g protein, 38g carbohydrates, 4g fat, 6g fiber, 0mg cholesterol, 70mg sodium, 500mg potassium.

6. Cauliflower Buffalo Bites

 Yield: 4 servings   **Prep time:** 10 minutes   **Cook time:** 15 minutes   **Cooking Temperature:** 400°F (200°C)   **Cooking Method:** Fry

Ingredients:

- 1 head cauliflower, cut into florets
- 1/2 cup buffalo sauce
- 1/2 cup breadcrumbs
- 1 tablespoon olive oil

Directions:

1. Preheat the air fryer to 400°F (200°C).
2. In a bowl, toss cauliflower florets with buffalo sauce and olive oil.
3. Coat with breadcrumbs and place in the air fryer basket.
4. Cook for 15 minutes, shaking halfway.

Nutritional Information

150 calories, 4g protein, 15g carbohydrates, 8g fat, 4g fiber, 0mg cholesterol, 350mg sodium, 300mg potassium.

7. Vegetable Samosas

 Yield:
6 servings

 Prep time:
15 minutes

 Cook time:
20 minutes

 Cooking Temperature:
375°F (190°C)

Cooking Method:
Fry

Ingredients:

- 1 package of pre-made samosa pastry
- 2 cups mixed vegetables (peas, carrots, potatoes)
- 1 tablespoon curry powder
- Salt to taste

Nutritional Information

180 calories, 4g protein, 28g carbohydrates, 6g fat, 2g fiber, 0mg cholesterol, 220mg sodium, 350mg potassium.

Directions:

1. Preheat the air fryer to 375°F (190°C).
2. In a bowl, mix mixed vegetables, curry powder, and salt.
3. Fill samosa pastry with the mixture and seal.
4. Place in the air fryer basket and cook for 20 minutes.

8. Falafel

 Yield:
4 servings

 Prep time:
10 minutes

 Cook time:
15 minutes

 Cooking Temperature:
380°F (190°C)

 Cooking Method:
Fry

Ingredients:

- 1 can (15 oz) chickpeas, drained and rinsed
- 1/4 cup parsley, chopped
- 1/4 cup onion, diced
- 1 teaspoon cumin
- Salt and pepper to taste

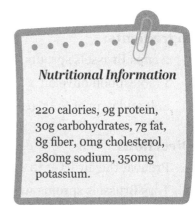

Nutritional Information

220 calories, 9g protein, 30g carbohydrates, 7g fat, 8g fiber, 0mg cholesterol, 280mg sodium, 350mg potassium.

Directions:

1. Preheat the air fryer to 380°F (190°C).
2. In a food processor, blend chickpeas, parsley, onion, cumin, salt, and pepper until coarse.
3. Form mixture into small balls and place in the air fryer basket.
4. Cook for 15 minutes, flipping halfway.

9. Portobello Mushroom Burgers

 Yield:
2 servings
 Prep time:
5 minutes
 Cook time:
10 minutes
Cooking Temperature:
400°F (200°C)
 Cooking Method:
Fry

Ingredients:

- 2 large portobello mushrooms
- 2 tablespoons balsamic vinegar
- 2 tablespoons olive oil
- Salt and pepper to taste

Nutritional Information

120 calories, 2g protein, 8g carbohydrates, 9g fat, 3g fiber, 0mg cholesterol, 5mg sodium, 300mg potassium.

Directions:

1. Preheat the air fryer to 400°F (200°C).
2. Brush portobello mushrooms with balsamic vinegar, olive oil, salt, and pepper.
3. Place in the air fryer basket.
4. Cook for 10 minutes.

10. Roasted Brussels Sprouts

 Yield:
4 servings
 Prep time:
5 minutes
 Cook time:
15 minutes
 Cooking Temperature:
400°F (200°C)
 Cooking Method:
Fry

Ingredients:

- 2 cups Brussels sprouts, halved
- 1 tablespoon olive oil
- Salt and pepper to taste

Nutritional Information

120 calories, 5g protein, 10g carbohydrates, 7g fat, 4g fiber, 0mg cholesterol, 30mg sodium, 400mg potassium.

Directions:

1. Preheat the air fryer to 400°F (200°C).
2. Toss Brussels sprouts with olive oil, salt, and pepper.
3. Place in the air fryer basket.
4. Cook for 15 minutes, shaking halfway.

11. Butternut Squash

 Yield:
4 servings

 Prep time:
10 minutes

 Cook time:
25 minutes

 Cooking Temperature:
400°F (200°C)

Cooking Method:
Fry

Ingredients:

- 1 medium butternut squash, peeled and cubed
- 2 tablespoons olive oil
- 1 teaspoon cinnamon
- Salt to taste

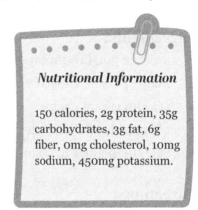

Nutritional Information

150 calories, 2g protein, 35g carbohydrates, 3g fat, 6g fiber, 0mg cholesterol, 10mg sodium, 450mg potassium.

Directions:

1. Preheat the air fryer to 400°F (200°C).
2. Toss butternut squash cubes with olive oil, cinnamon, and salt.
3. Place in the air fryer basket.
4. Cook for 25 minutes, shaking halfway.

12. Ratatouille

 Yield:
4 servings

 Prep time:
10 minutes

 Cook time:
20 minutes

 Cooking Temperature:
380°F (190°C)

Cooking Method:
Bake

Ingredients:

- 1 zucchini, diced
- 1 eggplant, diced
- 1 bell pepper, diced
- 1 can diced tomatoes (15 oz)
- 1 teaspoon Italian seasoning
- Salt and pepper to taste

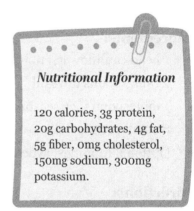

Nutritional Information

120 calories, 3g protein, 20g carbohydrates, 4g fat, 5g fiber, 0mg cholesterol, 150mg sodium, 300mg potassium.

Directions:

1. Preheat the air fryer to 380°F (190°C).
2. In a bowl, mix all the vegetables, diced tomatoes, Italian seasoning, salt, and pepper.
3. Place the mixture in a baking dish that fits in the air fryer.
4. Cook for 20 minutes, stirring halfway.

13. Spinach and Cheese Stuffed Mushrooms

 Yield:
4 servings

 Prep time:
10 minutes

 Cook time:
12 minutes

 Cooking Temperature:
375°F (190°C)

 Cooking Method:
Fry

Ingredients:

- 12 large mushroom caps
- 1 cup spinach, cooked and chopped
- 1/2 cup cream cheese
- 1/4 cup shredded cheese (mozzarella or cheddar)
- Salt and pepper to taste

Directions:

1. Preheat the air fryer to 375°F (190°C).
2. In a bowl, mix spinach, cream cheese, shredded cheese, salt, and pepper.
3. Stuff each mushroom cap with the mixture.
4. Place in the air fryer basket and cook for 12 minutes.

Nutritional Information

180 calories, 8g protein, 5g carbohydrates, 15g fat, 3g fiber, 30mg cholesterol, 250mg sodium, 350mg potassium.

14. Cauliflower Tacos

 Yield:
4 servings

 Prep time:
10 minutes

 Cook time:
15 minutes

 Cooking Temperature:
400°F (200°C)

 Cooking Method:
Fry

Ingredients:

- 1 head cauliflower, cut into small florets
- 2 tablespoons olive oil
- 1 tablespoon taco seasoning
- 8 small corn tortillas
- Optional toppings: avocado, salsa, cilantro

Directions:

1. Preheat the air fryer to 400°F (200°C).
2. Toss cauliflower florets with olive oil and taco seasoning.
3. Place in the air fryer basket and cook for 15 minutes.
4. Serve in corn tortillas with optional toppings.

Nutritional Information

220 calories, 5g protein, 34g carbohydrates, 10g fat, 10g fiber, 0mg cholesterol, 150mg sodium, 400mg potassium.

15. Baked Potatoes

 Yield:
4 servings

 Prep time:
5 minutes

 Cook time:
35 minutes

 Cooking Temperature:
400°F (200°C)

 Cooking Method:
Bake

Ingredients:
- 4 medium russet potatoes
- 1 tablespoon olive oil
- Salt and pepper to taste

Directions:
1. Preheat the air fryer to 400°F (200°C).
2. Rub potatoes with olive oil, salt, and pepper.
3. Prick potatoes with a fork and place in the air fryer basket.
4. Cook for 35 minutes, turning halfway.

Nutritional Information

160 calories, 4g protein, 37g carbohydrates, 0g fat, 4g fiber, 0mg cholesterol, 10mg sodium, 500mg potassium.

16. Grilled Vegetable Medley

 Yield:
4 servings

 Prep time:
10 minutes

 Cook time:
15 minutes

 Cooking Temperature:
400°F (200°C)

 Cooking Method:
Fry

Ingredients:
- 1 zucchini, sliced
- 1 bell pepper, sliced
- 1 red onion, sliced
- 2 tablespoons olive oil
- Salt and pepper to taste

Directions:
1. Preheat the air fryer to 400°F (200°C).
2. Toss vegetables with olive oil, salt, and pepper.
3. Place in the air fryer basket.
4. Cook for 15 minutes, shaking halfway.

Nutritional Information

120 calories, 3g protein, 15g carbohydrates, 6g fat, 4g fiber, 0mg cholesterol, 60mg sodium, 300mg potassium.

17. Vegetable Spring Rolls

 Yield:
4 servings

 Prep time:
15 minutes

 Cook time:
12 minutes

 Cooking Temperature:
400°F (200°C)

 Cooking Method:
Fry

Ingredients:

- 8 spring roll wrappers
- 2 cups mixed vegetables (carrots, cabbage, bell pepper)
- 1 tablespoon soy sauce
- 1 tablespoon sesame oil

Nutritional Information

180 calories, 4g protein, 30g carbohydrates, 6g fat, 3g fiber, 0mg cholesterol, 300mg sodium, 250mg potassium.

Directions:

1. Preheat the air fryer to 400°F (200°C).
2. In a bowl, mix vegetables, soy sauce, and sesame oil.
3. Fill spring roll wrappers with the mixture and roll tightly.
4. Place in the air fryer basket and cook for 12 minutes.

18. Quinoa and Black Bean Bowl

 Yield:
4 servings

 Prep time:
10 minutes

 Cook time:
15 minutes

 Cooking Temperature:
360°F (180°C)

 Cooking Method:
Bake

Ingredients:

- 1 cup cooked quinoa
- 1 can (15 oz) black beans, drained and rinsed
- 1 cup corn
- 1/2 cup salsa
- 1 teaspoon cumin

Nutritional Information

220 calories, 10g protein, 35g carbohydrates, 4g fat, 7g fiber, 0mg cholesterol, 200mg sodium, 400mg potassium.

Directions:

1. Preheat the air fryer to 360°F (180°C).
2. In a bowl, mix quinoa, black beans, corn, salsa, and cumin.
3. Place the mixture in a small baking dish that fits in the air fryer.
4. Cook for 15 minutes until heated through.

19. Chocolate-Covered Banana Bites

 Yield:
4 servings

 Prep time:
10 minutes

 Cook time:
5 minutes

 Cooking Temperature:
400°F (200°C)

 Cooking Method:
Fry

Ingredients:
- 2 bananas, sliced
- 1/2 cup dark chocolate chips
- 1 tablespoon coconut oil

Directions:
1. Preheat the air fryer to 400°F (200°C).
2. Melt chocolate chips with coconut oil in the microwave.
3. Dip banana slices in the chocolate and place in the air fryer basket.
4. Cook for 5 minutes until chocolate is set.

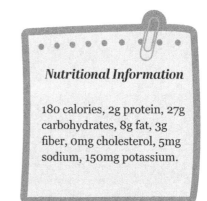

Nutritional Information

180 calories, 2g protein, 27g carbohydrates, 8g fat, 3g fiber, 0mg cholesterol, 5mg sodium, 150mg potassium.

20. Cauliflower Rice

 Yield:
4 servings

 Prep time:
5 minutes

 Cook time:
10 minutes

 Cooking Temperature:
400°F (200°C)

 Cooking Method:
Fry

Ingredients:
- 1 head cauliflower, grated into rice
- 2 tablespoons olive oil
- Salt and pepper to taste
- 1/2 teaspoon garlic powder

Directions:
1. Preheat the air fryer to 400°F (200°C).
2. Toss cauliflower rice with olive oil, salt, pepper, and garlic powder.
3. Place in the air fryer basket.
4. Cook for 10 minutes, shaking halfway.

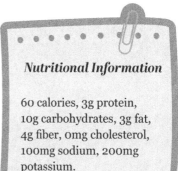

Nutritional Information

60 calories, 3g protein, 10g carbohydrates, 3g fat, 4g fiber, 0mg cholesterol, 100mg sodium, 200mg potassium.

Chapter 10

Snacks and Appetizers

1. Zucchini Fries

Yield: 4 servings

Prep time: 5 minutes

Cook time: 12 minutes

Cooking Temperature: 400°F (200°C)

Cooking Method: Fry

Ingredients:

- 2 medium zucchinis, cut into sticks
- 1/2 cup grated Parmesan cheese
- 1/2 cup panko breadcrumbs
- 1/2 tsp garlic powder
- Cooking spray

Nutritional Information

85 calories, 5g protein, 7g carbohydrates, 4g fat, 1g fiber, 8mg cholesterol, 160mg sodium, 250mg potassium.

Directions:

1. Mix Parmesan, breadcrumbs, and garlic powder in a bowl.
2. Coat zucchini sticks with breadcrumb mixture.
3. Place in the Air Fryer and spray with cooking spray.
4. Cook for 12 minutes or until crispy.

2. Buffalo Cauliflower Bites

Yield: 4 servings

Prep time: 5 minutes

Cook time: 15 minutes

Cooking Temperature: 375°F (190°C)

Cooking Method: Fry

Ingredients:

- 1 head cauliflower, cut into florets
- 1/2 cup hot sauce
- 1 tbsp olive oil
- Cooking spray

Nutritional Information

70 calories, 2g protein, 6g carbohydrates, 4g fat, 2g fiber, 0mg cholesterol, 200mg sodium, 320mg potassium.

Directions:

1. Toss cauliflower florets in hot sauce and olive oil.
2. Place cauliflower in Air Fryer basket in a single layer.
3. Cook for 15 minutes, shaking halfway through.

3. Sweet Potato Wedges

 Yield:
4 servings

 Prep time:
5 minutes

 Cook time:
18 minutes

 Cooking Temperature:
400°F (200°C)

 Cooking Method:
Fry

Ingredients:
- 2 medium sweet potatoes, cut into wedges
- 1 tbsp olive oil
- 1/2 tsp paprika
- 1/2 tsp salt

Directions:
1. Toss sweet potato wedges in olive oil, paprika, and salt.
2. Place wedges in the Air Fryer basket.
3. Cook for 18 minutes, shaking halfway.

Nutritional Information

105 calories, 1g protein, 20g carbohydrates, 3.5g fat, 3g fiber, 0mg cholesterol, 180mg sodium, 440mg potassium.

4. Chickpeas

 Yield:
3 servings

 Prep time:
2 minutes

 Cook time:
15 minutes

 Cooking Temperature:
375°F (190°C)

 Cooking Method:
Roast

Ingredients:
- 1 can (15 oz) chickpeas, drained and rinsed
- 1 tbsp olive oil
- 1/2 tsp cumin
- 1/2 tsp smoked paprika

Nutritional Information

120 calories, 5g protein, 18g carbohydrates, 4g fat, 4g fiber, 0mg cholesterol, 300mg sodium, 220mg potassium.

Directions:
1. Toss chickpeas with olive oil, cumin, and smoked paprika.
2. Spread evenly in the Air Fryer basket.
3. Roast for 15 minutes, shaking halfway through.

5. Mozzarella Sticks

 Yield:
4 servings

 Prep time:
5 minutes

 Cook time:
8 minutes

 Cooking Temperature:
375°F (190°C)

 Cooking Method:
Fry

Ingredients:

- 8 mozzarella sticks (low-fat)
- 1/2 cup panko breadcrumbs
- 1/4 tsp Italian seasoning
- Cooking spray

Nutritional Information

110 calories, 7g protein, 9g carbohydrates, 6g fat, 0g fiber, 18mg cholesterol, 170mg sodium, 30mg potassium.

Directions:

1. Coat mozzarella sticks with breadcrumbs mixed with Italian seasoning.
2. Freeze for 10 minutes.
3. Place in the Air Fryer and cook for 8 minutes, spraying lightly with cooking spray.

6. Stuffed Mushrooms

 Yield:
4 servings

 Prep time:
7 minutes

 Cook time:
10 minutes

 Cooking Temperature:
375°F (190°C)

 Cooking Method:
Bake

Ingredients:

- 8 large mushrooms, stems removed
- 1/4 cup cream cheese (reduced-fat)
- 2 tbsp grated Parmesan cheese
- 1 clove garlic, minced

Nutritional Information

85 calories, 4g protein, 4g carbohydrates, 1g fiber, 14mg cholesterol, 160mg sodium, 190mg potassium.

Directions:

1. Mix cream cheese, Parmesan, and minced garlic.
2. Stuff mushrooms with the cheese mixture.
3. Place in the Air Fryer and bake for 10 minutes.

7. Crispy Tofu Bites

 Yield:
4 servings

 Prep time:
5 minutes

 Cook time:
14 minutes

 Cooking Temperature:
400°F (200°C)

 Cooking Method:
Fry

Ingredients:

- 1 block (14 oz) extra-firm tofu, cubed
- 1 tbsp soy sauce (low-sodium)
- 1 tbsp cornstarch
- Cooking spray

Directions:

1. Toss tofu cubes with soy sauce and cornstarch.
2. Arrange tofu in the Air Fryer in a single layer.
3. Cook for 14 minutes, shaking halfway.

Nutritional Information

95 calories, 8g protein, 3g carbohydrates, 5g fat, 1g fiber, 0mg cholesterol, 300mg sodium, 150mg potassium.

8. Onion Rings

 Yield:
4 servings

 Prep time:
8 minutes

 Cook time:
10 minutes

 Cooking Temperature:
375°F (190°C)

 Cooking Method:
Fry

Ingredients:

- 1 large onion, sliced into rings
- 1/2 cup panko breadcrumbs
- 1/4 cup flour
- 1/2 cup buttermilk (low-fat)

Directions:

1. Dip onion rings in flour, then buttermilk, and coat with breadcrumbs.
2. Place in the Air Fryer in a single layer.
3. Cook for 10 minutes, flipping halfway.

Nutritional Information

90 calories, 2g protein, 15g carbohydrates, 2.5g fat, 1g fiber, 2mg cholesterol, 150mg sodium, 120mg potassium.

9. Jalapeno Poppers

 Yield:
4 servings

 Prep time:
5 minutes

 Cook time:
10 minutes

 Cooking Temperature:
375°F (190°C)

 Cooking Method:
Bake

Ingredients:
- 8 jalapenos, halved and seeded
- 1/4 cup cream cheese (low-fat)
- 1/4 cup shredded cheddar cheese
- Cooking spray

Directions:
1. Mix cream cheese and cheddar cheese, then stuff jalapenos.
2. Arrange stuffed jalapenos in the Air Fryer.
3. Cook for 10 minutes, until cheese is melted.

Nutritional Information

75 calories, 3g protein, 4g carbohydrates, 5g fat, 1g fiber, 10mg cholesterol, 100mg sodium, 90mg potassium.

10. Garlic Parmesan Shrimp

 Yield:
4 servings

 Prep time:
5 minutes

 Cook time:
8 minutes

 Cooking Temperature:
375°F (190°C)

 Cooking Method:
Fry

Ingredients:
- 1 lb shrimp, peeled and deveined
- 2 tbsp grated Parmesan cheese
- 1 tbsp olive oil
- 1/2 tsp garlic powder

Directions:
1. Toss shrimp with olive oil, Parmesan, and garlic powder.
2. Arrange shrimp in the Air Fryer basket in a single layer.
3. Cook for 8 minutes or until shrimp turn pink.

Nutritional Information

95 calories, 18g protein, 1g carbohydrates, 4g fat, 0g fiber, 85mg cholesterol, 220mg sodium, 180mg potassium.

11. Spiced Apple Chips

 Yield:
4 servings

 Prep time:
5 minutes

 Cook time:
15 minutes

 Cooking Temperature:
350°F (175°C)

 Cooking Method:
Bake

Ingredients:

- 2 large apples, thinly sliced
- 1/2 tsp cinnamon
- Cooking spray

Directions:

1. Toss apple slices with cinnamon.
2. Spread evenly in the Air Fryer basket.
3. Bake for 15 minutes, shaking halfway.

Nutritional Information

50 calories, 0g protein, 13g carbohydrates, 0g fat, 2g fiber, 0mg cholesterol, 0mg sodium, 100mg potassium.

12. Garlic Green Beans

 Yield:
4 servings

 Prep time:
3 minutes

 Cook time:
8 minutes

 Cooking Temperature:
375°F (190°C)

 Cooking Method:
Roast

Ingredients:

- 1 lb green beans, trimmed
- 1 tbsp olive oil
- 1/2 tsp garlic powder
- 1/4 tsp salt

Nutritional Information

60 calories, 2g protein, 7g carbohydrates, 3g fat, 3g fiber, 0mg cholesterol, 150mg sodium, 230mg potassium.

Directions:

1. Toss green beans with olive oil, garlic powder, and salt.
2. Place beans in the Air Fryer basket in a single layer.
3. Roast for 8 minutes, shaking halfway.

13. Cauliflower Tots

 Yield:
4 servings

 Prep time:
5 minutes

 Cook time:
10 minutes

 Cooking Temperature:
375°F (190°C)

 Cooking Method:
Fry

Ingredients:

- 2 cups riced cauliflower
- 1/4 cup grated Parmesan cheese
- 1 large egg
- 1/4 tsp garlic powder

Directions:

1. Mix cauliflower, Parmesan, egg, and garlic powder.
2. Form mixture into small tots.
3. Place tots in the Air Fryer basket and cook for 10 minutes, turning halfway.

Nutritional Information

70 calories, 5g protein, 4g carbohydrates, 4g fat, 2g fiber, 20mg cholesterol, 100mg sodium, 180mg potassium.

14. Falafel Bites

 Yield:
4 servings

 Prep time:
5 minutes

 Cook time:
12 minutes

 Cooking Temperature:
375°F (190°C)

 Cooking Method:
Fry

Ingredients:

- 1 can (15 oz) chickpeas, drained and rinsed
- 1/2 cup chopped onion
- 1/4 cup chopped parsley
- 1 tsp cumin

Directions:

1. Pulse chickpeas, onion, parsley, and cumin in a food processor.
2. Form mixture into small balls.
3. Place in the Air Fryer and cook for 12 minutes, flipping halfway.

Nutritional Information

100 calories, 4g protein, 15g carbohydrates, 3g fat, 4g fiber, 0mg cholesterol, 150mg sodium, 160mg potassium.

15. Eggplant Chips

 Yield:
4 servings

 Prep time:
3 minutes

 Cook time:
15 minutes

 Cooking Temperature:
400°F (200°C)

 Cooking Method:
Bake

Ingredients:

- 1 medium eggplant, sliced thinly
- 1 tbsp olive oil
- 1/2 tsp sea salt

Directions:

1. Toss eggplant slices with olive oil and sea salt.
2. Arrange slices in a single layer in the Air Fryer.
3. Bake for 15 minutes, flipping halfway through.

Nutritional Information

50 calories, 1g protein, 6g carbohydrates, 2.5g fat, 3g fiber, 0mg cholesterol, 120mg sodium, 200mg potassium.

16. Spinach & Cheese Stuffed Peppers

 Yield:
4 servings

 Prep time:
6 minutes

 Cook time:
10 minutes

 Cooking Temperature:
375°F (190°C)

 Cooking Method:
Bake

Ingredients:

- 8 mini bell peppers, halved and seeded
- 1/4 cup ricotta cheese (low-fat)
- 1/4 cup shredded mozzarella cheese
- 1/4 cup chopped spinach

Directions:

1. Mix ricotta, mozzarella, and chopped spinach.
2. Stuff peppers with the cheese mixture.
3. Place in the Air Fryer and bake for 10 minutes.

Nutritional Information

70 calories, 4g protein, 3g carbohydrates, 4g fat, 1g fiber, 10mg cholesterol, 100mg sodium, 100mg potassium.

17. Pita Chips

 Yield:
4 servings

 Prep time:
2 minutes

 Cook time:
7 minutes

 Cooking Temperature:
375°F (190°C)

 Cooking Method:
Bake

Ingredients:

- 2 whole wheat pitas, cut into wedges
- 1 tbsp olive oil
- 1/2 tsp dried oregano

Directions:

1. Toss pita wedges with olive oil and oregano.
2. Spread in a single layer in the Air Fryer.
3. Bake for 7 minutes or until crispy.

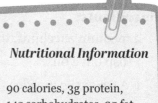

Nutritional Information

90 calories, 3g protein, 14g carbohydrates, 3g fat, 2g fiber, 0mg cholesterol, 120mg sodium, 80mg potassium.

18. Lemon Pepper Asparagus

 Yield:
4 servings

 Prep time:
3 minutes

 Cook time:
8 minutes

 Cooking Temperature:
375°F (190°C)

 Cooking Method:
Roast

Ingredients:

- 1 lb asparagus, trimmed
- 1 tbsp olive oil
- 1/2 tsp lemon pepper seasoning

Directions:

1. Toss asparagus with olive oil and lemon pepper seasoning.
2. Spread evenly in the Air Fryer basket.
3. Roast for 8 minutes, shaking halfway.

Nutritional Information

55 calories, 2g protein, 4g carbohydrates, 3g fat, 2g fiber, 0mg cholesterol, 90mg sodium, 230mg potassium.

19. Zucchini Chips

 Yield:
4 servings

 Prep time:
5 minutes

 Cook time:
12 minutes

 Cooking Temperature:
400°F (200°C)

 Cooking Method:
Bake

Ingredients:
- 2 medium zucchinis, thinly sliced
- 1 tbsp olive oil
- 1/2 tsp garlic powder

Directions:
1. Toss zucchini slices with olive oil and garlic powder.
2. Place in a single layer in the Air Fryer.
3. Bake for 12 minutes, flipping halfway.

Nutritional Information

60 calories, 1g protein, 5g carbohydrates, 4g fat, 1g fiber, 0mg cholesterol, 90mg sodium, 180mg potassium.

20. Spicy Edamame

 Yield:
4 servings

 Prep time:
2 minutes

 Cook time:
8 minutes

 Cooking Temperature:
375°F (190°C)

 Cooking Method:
Roast

Ingredients:
- 2 cups shelled edamame
- 1 tbsp soy sauce (low-sodium)
- 1/2 tsp crushed red pepper flakes

Directions:
1. Toss edamame with soy sauce and red pepper flakes.
2. Place in the Air Fryer basket in a single layer.
3. Roast for 8 minutes, shaking halfway.

Nutritional Information

95 calories, 9g protein, 6g carbohydrates, 4g fat, 3g fiber, 0mg cholesterol, 240mg sodium, 210mg potassium.

Chapter 11

Desserts

1. Apple Chips

 Yield:
4 servings

 Prep time:
5 minutes

 Cook time:
12 minutes

 Cooking Temperature:
350°F (175°C)

 Cooking Method:
Bake

Ingredients:

- 2 large apples, thinly sliced
- 1 tsp ground cinnamon

Directions:

1. Toss apple slices with cinnamon.
2. Place in the Air Fryer in a single layer.
3. Bake for 12 minutes, flipping halfway.

Nutritional Information

50 calories, 0g protein, 14g carbohydrates, 0g fat, 3g fiber, 0mg cholesterol, 0mg sodium, 150mg potassium.

2. Banana Chips

 Yield:
4 servings

 Prep time:
5 minutes

 Cook time:
10 minutes

 Cooking Temperature:
350°F (175°C)

 Cooking Method:
Bake

Ingredients:

- 2 large bananas, thinly sliced
- 1 tsp olive oil
- 1 tsp honey (optional)

Directions:

1. Toss banana slices with olive oil and honey (if using).
2. Arrange in the Air Fryer basket.
3. Bake for 10 minutes, shaking halfway.

Nutritional Information

75 calories, 1g protein, 19g carbohydrates, 1g fat, 2g fiber, 0mg cholesterol, 0mg sodium, 200mg potassium.

3. Baked Apples

 Yield:
4 servings

 Prep time:
5 minutes

 Cook time:
15 minutes

 Cooking Temperature:
350°F (190°C)

 Cooking Method:
Bake

Ingredients:
- 4 medium apples, cored
- 2 tbsp maple syrup
- 1/2 tsp ground cinnamon

Directions:
1. Core apples and drizzle with maple syrup and cinnamon.
2. Place apples in the Air Fryer.
3. Bake for 15 minutes or until soft.

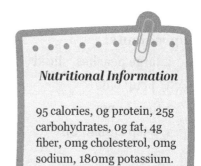

Nutritional Information

95 calories, 0g protein, 25g carbohydrates, 0g fat, 4g fiber, 0mg cholesterol, 0mg sodium, 180mg potassium.

4. Chocolate-Covered Strawberries

 Yield:
4 servings

 Prep time:
5 minutes

 Cook time:
5 minutes

 Cooking Temperature:
320°F (160°C)

 Cooking Method:
Bake

Ingredients:
- 12 large strawberries
- 1/4 cup dark chocolate chips
- 1 tsp coconut oil

Directions:
1. Melt chocolate chips and coconut oil in the Air Fryer.
2. Dip strawberries in melted chocolate.
3. Let chill in the fridge for 5 minutes before serving.

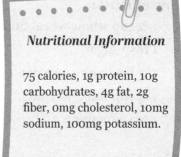

Nutritional Information

75 calories, 1g protein, 10g carbohydrates, 4g fat, 2g fiber, 0mg cholesterol, 10mg sodium, 100mg potassium.

5. Peach Crisp

 Yield:
4 servings

 Prep time:
5 minutes

 Cook time:
12 minutes

 Cooking Temperature:
350°F (175°C)

 Cooking Method:
Bake

Ingredients:

- 2 large peaches, sliced
- 1/4 cup oats
- 1 tbsp honey
- 1/2 tsp cinnamon

Directions:

1. Toss peach slices with honey and cinnamon.
2. Top with oats and place in the Air Fryer.
3. Bake for 12 minutes.

Nutritional Information

120 calories, 2g protein, 25g carbohydrates, 3g fat, 3g fiber, 0mg cholesterol, 5mg sodium, 250mg potassium.

6. Cinnamon Sugar Donuts

 Yield:
4 servings

 Prep time:
7 minutes

 Cook time:
10 minutes

 Cooking Temperature:
350°F (175°C)

 Cooking Method:
Bake

Ingredients:

- 1/2 cup whole wheat flour
- 1 tbsp sugar
- 1/2 tsp baking powder
- 1/4 cup milk (low-fat)
- 1 tsp cinnamon

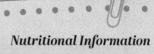

Nutritional Information

95 calories, 3g protein, 18g carbohydrates, 1g fat, 1g fiber, 0mg cholesterol, 100mg sodium, 50mg potassium.

Directions:

1. Mix flour, sugar, baking powder, and milk into a dough.
2. Shape dough into small donuts.
3. Bake in the Air Fryer for 10 minutes, then dust with cinnamon.

7. Coconut Macaroons

 Yield:
4 servings

 Prep time:
5 minutes

 Cook time:
8 minutes

 Cooking Temperature:
325°F (160°C)

 Cooking Method:
Bake

Ingredients:

- 1 cup shredded coconut (unsweetened)
- 1/4 cup egg whites
- 1 tbsp honey

Directions:

1. Mix coconut, egg whites, and honey.
2. Shape into small mounds.
3. Bake for 8 minutes.

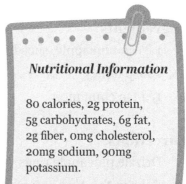

Nutritional Information

80 calories, 2g protein, 5g carbohydrates, 6g fat, 2g fiber, 0mg cholesterol, 20mg sodium, 90mg potassium.

8. Blueberry Muffins

 Yield:
4 servings

 Prep time:
7 minutes

 Cook time:
12 minutes

 Cooking Temperature:
350°F (175°C)

 Cooking Method:
Bake

Ingredients:

- 1 cup whole wheat flour
- 1/4 cup blueberries
- 1/4 cup almond milk
- 1 tbsp honey
- 1/2 tsp baking powder

Directions:

1. Mix all ingredients into a batter.
2. Pour into small muffin molds.
3. Bake for 12 minutes in the Air Fryer.

Nutritional Information

110 calories, 4g protein, 20g carbohydrates, 3g fat, 2g fiber, 0mg cholesterol, 120mg sodium, 150mg potassium.

9. Pineapple Rings

 Yield:
4 servings

 Prep time:
5 minutes

 Cook time:
10 minutes

 Cooking Temperature:
350°F (175°C)

 Cooking Method:
Bake

Ingredients:
- 1 fresh pineapple, sliced into rings
- 1 tbsp honey
- 1/2 tsp cinnamon

Directions:
1. Drizzle pineapple rings with honey and cinnamon.
2. Bake in the Air Fryer for 10 minutes.

Nutritional Information

85 calories, 1g protein, 22g carbohydrates, 0g fat, 2g fiber, 0mg cholesterol, 5mg sodium, 180mg potassium.

10. Pear Crumble

 Yield:
4 servings

 Prep time:
5 minutes

 Cook time:
12 minutes

 Cooking Temperature:
350°F (175°C)

 Cooking Method:
Bake

Ingredients:
- 2 large pears, sliced
- 1/4 cup oats
- 1 tbsp maple syrup
- 1/4 tsp nutmeg

Directions:
1. Toss pear slices with maple syrup and nutmeg.
2. Top with oats and bake for 12 minutes.

Nutritional Information

110 calories, 2g protein, 24g carbohydrates, 2g fat, 4g fiber, 0mg cholesterol, 0mg sodium, 200mg potassium.

11. Churro Bites

 Yield:
4 servings

 Prep time:
7 minutes

 Cook time:
8 minutes

 Cooking Temperature:
350°F (175°C)

 Cooking Method:
Fry

Ingredients:

- 1/2 cup flour
- 1 tbsp sugar
- 1/2 tsp baking powder
- 1/4 cup almond milk
- 1 tsp cinnamon

Nutritional Information

100 calories, 2g protein, 18g carbohydrates, 1g fat, 1g fiber, 0mg cholesterol, 110mg sodium, 50mg potassium.

Directions:

1. Mix flour, sugar, baking powder, and milk into a dough.
2. Shape into small bites and fry for 8 minutes in the Air Fryer.

12. Pumpkin Spice Cookies

 Yield:
4 servings

 Prep time:
5 minutes

 Cook time:
10 minutes

 Cooking Temperature:
350°F (175°C)

 Cooking Method:
Bake

Ingredients:

- 1/2 cup pumpkin puree
- 1/2 cup oats
- 1 tbsp honey
- 1/2 tsp pumpkin spice

Nutritional Information

95 calories, 2g protein, 19g carbohydrates, 1.5g fat, 3g fiber, 0mg cholesterol, 5mg sodium, 150mg potassium.

Directions:

1. Mix pumpkin puree, oats, honey, and pumpkin spice.
2. Shape into small cookies.
3. Bake in the Air Fryer for 10 minutes.

13. Pear Chips

 Yield:
4 servings

 Prep time:
5 minutes

 Cook time:
12 minutes

 Cooking Temperature:
350°F (175°C)

 Cooking Method:
Bake

Ingredients:
- 2 large pears, thinly sliced
- 1/2 tsp cinnamon

Directions:
1. Sprinkle pear slices with cinnamon.
2. Arrange in the Air Fryer in a single layer.
3. Bake for 12 minutes, flipping halfway.

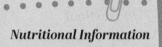

Nutritional Information

65 calories, 0g protein, 17g carbohydrates, 0g fat, 4g fiber, 0mg cholesterol, 0mg sodium, 150mg potassium.

14. Chocolate Chip Cookies

 Yield:
4 servings

 Prep time:
7 minutes

 Cook time:
8 minutes

 Cooking Temperature:
350°F (175°C)

 Cooking Method:
Bake

Ingredients:
- 1/4 cup whole wheat flour
- 2 tbsp brown sugar
- 1/8 tsp baking soda
- 2 tbsp chocolate chips
- 1 tbsp coconut oil

Directions:
1. Mix flour, sugar, baking soda, chocolate chips, and coconut oil.
2. Shape into small cookie balls.
3. Bake in the Air Fryer for 8 minutes.

Nutritional Information

115 calories, 1g protein, 15g carbohydrates, 6g fat, 1g fiber, 0mg cholesterol, 55mg sodium, 50mg potassium.

15. Cinnamon Roasted Pineapple

 Yield:
4 servings

 Prep time:
5 minutes

 Cook time:
10 minutes

 Cooking Temperature:
350°F (175°C)

 Cooking Method:
Roast

Ingredients:

- 1 medium pineapple, cut into chunks
- 1 tbsp brown sugar
- 1/2 tsp cinnamon

Directions:

1. Toss pineapple chunks with brown sugar and cinnamon.
2. Roast in the Air Fryer for 10 minutes, shaking halfway.

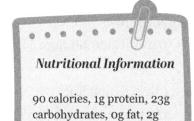

Nutritional Information

90 calories, 1g protein, 23g carbohydrates, 0g fat, 2g fiber, 0mg cholesterol, 5mg sodium, 180mg potassium.

16. Strawberry Shortcake Bites

 Yield:
4 servings

 Prep time:
5 minutes

 Cook time:
8 minutes

 Cooking Temperature:
350°F (175°C)

 Cooking Method:
Bake

Ingredients:

- 1/2 cup whole wheat flour
- 1/4 cup almond milk
- 1 tbsp honey
- 1/2 cup chopped strawberries

Nutritional Information

105 calories, 2g protein, 20g carbohydrates, 2.5g fat, 2g fiber, 0mg cholesterol, 55mg sodium, 100mg potassium.

Directions:

1. Mix flour, almond milk, and honey into a batter.
2. Fold in chopped strawberries.
3. Spoon batter into small molds and bake for 8 minutes.

17. Lemon Bars

 Yield:
4 servings

 Prep time:
5 minutes

 Cook time:
10 minutes

 Cooking Temperature:
325°F (160°C)

 Cooking Method:
Bake

Ingredients:

- 1/2 cup almond flour
- 2 tbsp honey
- 1 tbsp lemon juice
- 1/4 tsp lemon zest

Directions:

1. Mix almond flour, honey, lemon juice, and lemon zest into a dough.
2. Press into small molds and bake in the Air Fryer for 10 minutes.

Nutritional Information

90 calories, 2g protein, 10g carbohydrates, 5g fat, 1g fiber, 0mg cholesterol, 5mg sodium, 50mg potassium.

18. Banana Fritters

 Yield:
4 servings

 Prep time:
5 minutes

 Cook time:
8 minutes

 Cooking Temperature:
350°F (175°C)

 Cooking Method:
Fry

Ingredients:

- 1 large banana, mashed
- 1/4 cup whole wheat flour
- 1/2 tsp cinnamon
- 1 tbsp honey

Directions:

1. Mix mashed banana, flour, cinnamon, and honey.
2. Shape into small fritters.
3. Fry in the Air Fryer for 8 minutes.

Nutritional Information

85 calories, 1g protein, 18g carbohydrates, 1g fat, 2g fiber, 0mg cholesterol, 0mg sodium, 120mg potassium.

19. Chocolate Banana Bites

 Yield:
4 servings

 Prep time:
5 minutes

 Cook time:
5 minutes

 Cooking Temperature:
320°F (160°C)

 Cooking Method:
Bake

Ingredients:
- 1 large banana, sliced
- 2 tbsp dark chocolate chips
- 1 tsp coconut oil

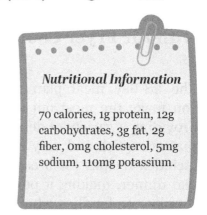

Nutritional Information

70 calories, 1g protein, 12g carbohydrates, 3g fat, 2g fiber, 0mg cholesterol, 5mg sodium, 110mg potassium.

Directions:
1. Melt chocolate chips and coconut oil in the Air Fryer.
2. Dip banana slices in melted chocolate.
3. Let chill in the fridge before serving.

20. Berry Cobbler

 Yield:
4 servings

 Prep time:
5 minutes

 Cook time:
10 minutes

 Cooking Temperature:
350°F (175°C)

 Cooking Method:
Bake

Ingredients:
- 1 cup mixed berries (blueberries, raspberries, strawberries)
- 1/4 cup oats
- 1 tbsp honey
- 1/2 tsp vanilla extract

Nutritional Information

95 calories, 1g protein, 20g carbohydrates, 1.5g fat, 3g fiber, 0mg cholesterol, 0mg sodium, 100mg potassium.

Directions:
1. Toss mixed berries with honey and vanilla.
2. Top with oats and place in the Air Fryer.
3. Bake for 10 minutes.

How to Use the 28-Day Meal Plan with Air Fryer Cooking

The 28-day meal plan is designed to help you make the most out of your Air Fryer by providing a variety of delicious, healthy meals that are quick and easy to prepare. The plan includes recipes for breakfast, snacks, lunch, and dinner, making it perfect for individuals, couples, or families who want to maintain a balanced diet while saving time in the kitchen. Here's how you can effectively use the meal plan:

1. Get Familiar with Your Air Fryer

Before you begin, make sure you understand the settings and capabilities of your Air Fryer. Familiarize yourself with the temperature and time settings, as many of the recipes provided in the meal plan require specific temperatures in both Fahrenheit and Celsius.

2. Meal Planning and Preparation

- **Weekly Preparation:** Each week, review the upcoming recipes for breakfast, snacks, lunch, and dinner. Take note of the ingredients needed and make a shopping list for the entire week. This will save time and ensure you have everything on hand.

- **Batch Prep:** Consider preparing certain ingredients in advance. For example, you can pre-chop vegetables, marinate proteins, or prepare mixes for dishes like fritters or falafel bites. This will make daily meal preparation much faster.

3. Utilize the "Dump and Go" Style Cooking

The meal plan is designed to be as hassle-free as possible, focusing on "dump and go" recipes. This means that most recipes require minimal preparation—you simply place the ingredients in the Air Fryer, set the temperature and time, and let it cook:

- **Breakfast:** Recipes like "Air Fryer French Toast Sticks" or "Air Fryer Egg Muffins" can be quickly prepared in the morning and cooked while you get ready for the day.

- **Snacks:** Keep snacks like "Air Fryer Zucchini Fries" or "Air Fryer Sweet Potato Wedges" handy for when hunger strikes between meals. These can be cooked in just a few minutes and are much healthier than processed snacks.

- **Lunch and Dinner:** Recipes like "Air Fryer Lemon Garlic Chicken Thighs" or "Air Fryer Stuffed Bell Peppers" are perfect for a satisfying lunch or dinner. Simply prepare the ingredients, place them in the Air Fryer, and allow them to cook while you take care of other tasks.

4. Stay Organized

- **Label and Store Ingredients:** Use labeled containers for prepped ingredients in your fridge. This will help you quickly grab what you need for each meal, minimizing time spent searching for ingredients.

- **Follow the Meal Plan Consistently:** The meal plan is structured to ensure variety and balanced nutrition. Following it consistently will help you make healthier choices and avoid repetitive meals.

5. Customize Based on Preferences

While the meal plan provides a variety of options, you can customize it based on your preferences:

- **Swap Ingredients:** Feel free to swap out vegetables, proteins, or seasonings based on your tastes or what's available in your pantry. For example, if a recipe calls for chicken and you have fish, you can substitute it and adjust the cooking time accordingly.

- **Adjust Portions:** The meal plan is suitable for a range of servings, from 2 to 6 people. Adjust the portions based on your household size, and use the Air Fryer basket capacity to determine how much can be cooked at once.

6. Cooking Tips for Air Fryer Success

- **Do Not Overcrowd the Basket:** To ensure even cooking, avoid overcrowding the Air Fryer basket. If you need to make larger portions, consider cooking in batches.

- **Use Cooking Spray:** For some recipes, a light spray of oil will help achieve a crispier texture. This is especially helpful for recipes like "Air Fryer Mozzarella Sticks" or "Air Fryer Onion Rings."

- **Shake the Basket:** For items like fries or chips, shake the basket halfway through cooking to ensure even crisping on all sides.

7. Stay Flexible

Life can be unpredictable, so feel free to swap meals around as needed. The meal plan is designed to provide flexibility. If you have leftovers from dinner, consider using them for lunch the next day. Many Air Fryer recipes reheat well, maintaining their crispy texture.

8. Track Your Progress

- **Keep a Journal:** Track which recipes you enjoyed the most and any modifications you made. This will help you build a collection of favorite go-to recipes for future weeks.

- **Observe Your Preferences:** After completing the 28-day plan, you'll have a better understanding of which meals fit your routine and tastes the best. Use this knowledge to customize your next meal plan for even more convenience.

9. Benefits of Using the Air Fryer Meal Plan

- **Healthy Eating Made Easy:** The recipes are designed to be low in calories and nutrient-dense, helping you maintain a healthy diet without sacrificing flavor.

- **Time-Saving:** Most meals can be prepared in under 30 minutes, allowing you to spend more time on other activities while your food cooks.

- **Less Cleaning:** Air Fryer cooking requires minimal oil, resulting in fewer greasy dishes to clean. This means less time spent scrubbing and more time enjoying your meal.

By following this 28-day Air Fryer meal plan, you'll enjoy a variety of nutritious meals that are simple to prepare and full of flavor. It's a great way to make healthy eating a regular part of your lifestyle while making the most out of your Air Fryer.

Here's a detailed 28-day meal plan using the provided recipes in the Book:

W1	Breakfast	Snack	Lunch	Dinner
SUN	Veggie Sausage Links (Page 16)	Falafel Bites (Page 103)	Apple Chips (Page 29)	Honey Garlic Chicken Wings (Page 37)
MON	Breakfast Quesadilla (Page 13)	Jalapeno Poppers (Page 101)	Chickpea Salad (Page 25)	Mini Pizza (Page 34)
TUE	French Toast Sticks (Page 13)	Zucchini Chips (Page 106)	Eggplant Parmesan (Page 25)	Spinach Artichoke Dip (Page 39)
WED	Cinnamon Apples (Page 11)	Spicy Edamame (Page 106)	Turkey Meatballs (Page 22)	Stuffed Bell Peppers (Page 22)
THU	Avocado Toast (Page 14)	Eggplant Chips (Page 104)	Lemon Garlic Chicken Thighs (Page 20)	Chicken Fajitas (Page 31)
FRI	Breakfast Burritos (Page 11)	Onion Rings (Page 100)	Garlic Parmesan Brussels Sprouts (Page 24)	Broccoli and Cheese Casserole (Page 23)
SAT	Cheesy Grits Casserole (Page 17)	Stuffed Mushrooms (Page 44)	Shrimp Tacos (Page 23)	Honey Mustard Chicken Drumsticks (Page 40)

W2	Breakfast	Snack	Lunch	Dinner
SUN	Banana Bread (Page 10)	Garlic Green Beans (Page 102)	Butternut Squash Soup (Page 26)	Sweet Potato Fries (Page 33)
MON	Breakfast Potatoes (Page 9)	Spiced Apple Chips (Page 102)	Broccoli and Cheese Casserole (Page 23)	Quinoa Salad (Page 36)
TUE	Breakfast Pita (Page 15)	Cauliflower Tots (Page 103)	Buffalo Cauliflower Bites (Page 97)	Salmon with Lemon (Page 33)
WED	Quinoa Breakfast Bowl (Page 18)	Crispy Tofu Bites (Page 100)	Stuffed Bell Peppers (Page 22)	Cabbage and Sausage Skillet (Page 37)
THU	Oatmeal Cups (Page 10)	Sweet Potato Wedges (Page 88)	Chicken and Broccoli (Page 27)	Vegetable Samosas (Page 36)
FRI	Ham and Egg Cups (Page 17)	Pita Chips (Page 105)	Lentil Tacos (Page 26)	Vegetable Quesadillas (Page 39)
SAT	Sweet Potato Hash (Page 15)	Lemon Pepper Asparagus (Page 105)	Teriyaki Salmon (Page 55)	BBQ Meatballs (Page 31)

W3	Breakfast	Snack	Lunch	Dinner
SUN	Chocolate Banana Oatmeal (Page 18)	Mozzarella Sticks (Page 99)	Zucchini Fritters (Page 20)	Coconut Shrimp (Page 40)
MON	Egg Muffins (Page 9)	Spinach & Cheese Stuffed Peppers (Page 104)	Roasted Carrots (Page 28)	Egg and Veggie Breakfast Bowls (Page 35)
TUE	Veggie Frittata (Page 12)	Garlic Parmesan Shrimp (Page 101)	Spinach and Feta Stuffed Chicken (Page 27)	Teriyaki Chicken (Page 32)
WED	Cottage Cheese Pancakes (Page 16)	Chickpeas (Page 98)	Pesto Chicken Breasts (Page 24)	Cheesy Broccoli Rice (Page 38)
THU	Chia Seed Pudding (Page 14)	Buffalo Cauliflower Bites (Page 97)	Cabbage Steaks (Page 29)	Turkey and Spinach Stuffed Peppers (Page 38)
FRI	Greek Yogurt Pancakes (Page 12)	Zucchini Fries (Page 86)	Pizza Rolls (Page 28)	Pork Chops (Page 35)
SAT	Banana Bread (Page 10)	Spicy Edamame (Page 106)	Eggplant Parmesan (Page 25)	Sweet Potato Fries (Page 33)

W4	Breakfast	Snack	Lunch	Dinner
SUN	Cinnamon Apples (Page 11)	Cauliflower Tots (Page 103)	Pesto Chicken Breasts (Page 24)	Pork Chops (Page 35)
MON	Breakfast Burritos (Page 11)	Garlic Parmesan Shrimp (Page 101)	Turkey Meatballs (Page 22)	Spinach Artichoke Dip (Page 39)
TUE	Breakfast Pita (Page 15)	Onion Rings (Page 100)	Lemon Garlic Chicken Thighs (Page 20)	Teriyaki Chicken (Page 32)
WED	Egg Muffins (Page 9)	Jalapeno Poppers (Page 101)	Shrimp Tacos (Page 23)	Cheesy Broccoli Rice (Page 38)
THU	Veggie Sausage Links (Page 16)	Stuffed Mushrooms (Page 44)	Chicken and Broccoli (Page 27)	Turkey and Spinach Stuffed Peppers (Page 38)
FRI	Sweet Potato Hash (Page 15)	Pita Chips (Page 105)	Stuffed Bell Peppers (Page 22)	Egg and Veggie Breakfast Bowls (Page 35)
SAT	Chia Seed Pudding (Page 14)	Lemon Pepper Asparagus (Page 105)	Butternut Squash Soup (Page 26)	Honey Garlic Chicken Wings (Page 37)

Here's an estimated shopping list with quantities for the 28-day meal plan, with each ingredient categorized and given appropriate units:

1. Vegetables & Fruits

Apples: 16 medium (for snacks and desserts)	**Bananas:** 12 large (for breakfast and desserts)	**Pears:** 6 medium (for snacks and desserts)
Peaches: 4 medium (for desserts)	**Strawberries:** 3 pints (for breakfasts and desserts)	**Blueberries:** 2 pints (for breakfasts and desserts)
Pineapple: 2 large (for snacks and desserts)	**Lemons:** 12 (for various dishes)	**Limes:** 6 (for seafood and dressings)
Oranges: 4 (for marinades and salads)	**Avocados:** 8 large (for breakfast and lunch)	**Sweet potatoes:** 10 medium (for breakfasts, sides, and snacks)
Russet potatoes: 8 medium (for breakfasts and sides)	**Baby potatoes:** 3 lbs (for sides)	**Zucchini:** 8 medium (for snacks, lunches, and sides)
Cauliflower: 4 heads (for snacks, sides, and main dishes)	**Broccoli:** 6 heads (for sides and lunches)	**Brussels sprouts:** 3 lbs (for sides and lunches)
Eggplant: 4 medium (for lunches and dinners)	**Bell peppers:** 12 (variety of colors; for breakfasts, lunches, and dinners)	**Cherry tomatoes:** 4 pints (for salads and lunches)
Red onions: 4 large (for salads and dinners)	**White onions:** 8 medium (for various dishes)	**Green beans:** 2 lbs (for snacks and sides)
Garlic cloves: 4 bulbs (for flavoring various dishes)	**Fresh spinach:** 4 bags (for breakfasts, lunches, and sides)	**Fresh parsley:** 2 bunches (for garnishing and salads)
Fresh basil: 2 bunches (for garnishing and main dishes)	**Mushrooms:** 3 lbs (for breakfasts, lunches, and dinners)	**Asparagus:** 3 lbs (for sides and dinners)
Carrots: 3 lbs (for snacks, lunches, and dinners)	**Jalapenos:** 8 (for snacks and main dishes)	**Lettuce (romaine or butter):** 4 heads (for wraps and salads)

2. Protein & Dairy

Chicken breasts: 14 lbs (for lunches and dinners)	**Chicken thighs:** 8 lbs (for dinners)	**Chicken drumsticks:** 10 (for dinners)
Lean ground turkey: 6 lbs (for lunches and dinners)	**Shrimp:** 6 lbs (for lunches and dinners)	**Salmon fillets:** 10 (for lunches and dinners)
Cod fillets: 8 (for dinners)	**Tilapia fillets:** 6 (for dinners)	**Beef (ground, stew meat, steaks):** 10 lbs (for dinners)
Lamb chops: 8 (for dinners)	**Pork chops:** 6 (for dinners)	**Bacon:** 2 packs (optional for breakfasts and dinners)
Eggs: 4 dozen (for breakfasts and baking)	**Greek yogurt:** 8 cups (for breakfasts and snacks)	**Cottage cheese:** 4 cups (for breakfasts)
Shredded mozzarella cheese: 4 cups (for various dishes)	**Parmesan cheese:** 2 cups (for various dishes)	**Cream cheese:** 1 block (for snacks and desserts)
Cheddar cheese: 4 cups (for various dishes)	**Feta cheese:** 2 cups (for salads and dishes)	

3. Pantry Staples

Whole wheat flour: 2 lbs (for baking and coating)	**All-purpose flour:** 2 lbs (for baking and coating)	**Panko breadcrumbs:** 1 box (for coating)
Oats: 2 lbs (for breakfasts and baking)	**Brown sugar:** 2 cups (for baking and desserts)	**White sugar:** 2 cups (for baking and desserts)
Honey: 1 jar (for marinades, desserts, and dressings)	**Maple syrup:** 1 bottle (for breakfasts and desserts)	**Baking powder:** 1 container (for baking)
Baking soda: 1 container (for baking)	**Cornstarch:** 1 container (for thickening)	**Olive oil:** 1 bottle (for cooking and roasting)
Coconut oil: 1 jar (for desserts and baking)	**Cooking spray:** 2 cans (for air fryer use)	**Soy sauce:** 1 bottle (for marinades)
Worcestershire sauce: 1 bottle (for marinades)	**Balsamic vinegar:** 1 bottle (for dressings)	**Apple cider vinegar:** 1 bottle (for dressings)
Dijon mustard: 1 jar (for dressings and marinades)	**Honey mustard:** 1 jar (optional)	**Tomato paste:** 4 cans (for sauces)
Canned chickpeas: 8 cans (for snacks and main dishes)	**Lentils:** 4 cans (for soups and main dishes)	**Canned black beans:** 6 cans (for various dishes)
Canned coconut milk: 4 cans (for curries and desserts)	**Fish sauce:** 1 bottle (for Asian-inspired dishes)	**Cornmeal:** 1 box (for coating and baking)
Salsa: 1 jar (optional)	**Crushed red pepper flakes:** 1 container (for seasoning)	

4. Grains, Pasta, & Bread

Tortilla wraps: 2 packs (for wraps)	**Pita bread:** 1 pack (for lunches)	**Rice:** 5 lbs (for side dishes)
Quinoa: 3 lbs (for side dishes)	**Pasta:** 3 lbs (for main dishes)	**Bread:** 2 loaves (for toasts and sandwiches)
Corn tortillas: 1 pack (for tacos)		

5. Spices & Seasonings

Salt: 1 box	**Black pepper:** 1 container	**Garlic powder:** 1 container
Onion powder: 1 container	**Smoked paprika:** 1 container	**Ground cumin:** 1 container
Ground coriander: 1 container	**Chili powder:** 1 container	**Cayenne pepper:** 1 container
Ground cinnamon: 1 container	**Pumpkin spice:** 1 container	**Ground nutmeg:** 1 container
Ground ginger: 1 container	**Dried thyme:** 1 container	**Dried rosemary:** 1 container
Italian seasoning: 1 container	**Dried oregano:** 1 container	**Turmeric:** 1 container

Cajun seasoning: 1 container	Lemon pepper seasoning: 1 container	
6. Canned Goods & Jars		
Canned crushed tomatoes: 8 cans (for sauces and dishes)	**Tomato sauce:** 4 cans (for dishes)	**Peanut butter or almond butter:** 1 jar (optional for snacks and desserts)
Dill pickles: 1 jar (optional)	**Canned tuna or salmon:** 4 cans (optional for variety)	
7. Miscellaneous & Snacks		
Dark chocolate chips: 2 bags (for desserts)	**Low-fat buttermilk:** 1 quart (for baking)	**Shredded coconut:** 1 bag (for desserts)
Low-sodium broth: 4 cartons (chicken, beef, or vegetable)	**Marinara sauce:** 2 jars (for pastas)	**Graham cracker crumbs:** 1 box (optional for desserts)
Coconut flakes: 1 bag (optional for desserts)	**Sesame seeds:** 1 container (for garnishing)	

This shopping list provides quantities based on the estimated usage across the 28-day meal plan. You may need to adjust some quantities depending on portion sizes and your family's preferences. This comprehensive list should help you have everything needed to create easy, healthy, and delicious meals using your Air Fryer!

Conclusion

Congratulations on taking the first step towards transforming your everyday meals into healthy, delicious, and effortless creations with your Air Fryer! Whether you're new to air frying or a seasoned enthusiast looking to expand your cooking repertoire, this cookbook has been crafted with you in mind. Packed with a variety of fast, simple, and mouthwatering recipes, it aims to make your culinary journey both enjoyable and convenient.

The Air Fryer has become a revolutionary kitchen appliance, allowing you to create a wide array of dishes—from savory breakfasts to indulgent desserts—with minimal oil, less time, and far fewer calories. With the 28-Day Meal Plan included, meal planning no longer needs to be stressful or time-consuming. You'll have a balanced, easy-to-follow guide to help you navigate each day, ensuring you have tasty meals that meet your health goals without compromising on flavor.

We've filled the cookbook with a diverse range of recipes to cater to all your culinary needs:

- **Fast and Easy Daily Favorites** for quick, wholesome meals.
- **Family-Friendly Recipes** that satisfy even the pickiest of eaters.
- **Perfect-for-Two Dishes** for intimate dinners.
- **Beef, Pork, Lamb, Fish, and Seafood Varieties** to bring diversity to your dining table.
- **Vegetarian Delights** that are satisfying and nutrient-dense.
- **Snacks and Desserts** that bring a touch of indulgence while staying low in calories, fat, and sodium.

The "Dump-and-Go" style recipes are designed to fit seamlessly into your busy lifestyle. Just throw in the ingredients, set the time and temperature, and let the Air Fryer work its magic. The versatility of the Air Fryer—whether you're frying, roasting, or baking—makes it the ideal companion for anyone seeking quick, healthy meals using simple pantry staples. No need for complex ingredients; everything is kept affordable and accessible.

Throughout this journey, you've learned how to make meals that are not only good for you but are also rich in flavor and texture. The ease of using your Air Fryer means less time spent in the kitchen and more time spent enjoying meals with your loved ones. The **Measurement Conversion Chart** and **Air Fryer Cooking Chart** included are handy references to help you achieve perfect results every time, making cooking even more convenient.

The addition of the **TWO Bonus e-books by Lisa Larsen** means you now have even more options at your fingertips to inspire your culinary creativity. These extra recipes are sure to bring variety and excitement to your kitchen, allowing you to explore new flavors and cooking techniques.

Whether you're cooking for yourself, your partner, or the entire family, this cookbook is here to provide you with simple, nutritious, and delicious meals every day. No matter the occasion, the recipes in this book are designed to help you make the most out of your Air Fryer—turning everyday ingredients into extraordinary dishes.

Thank you for making us part of your culinary adventure. We hope that this **Everyday Simple Air Fryer Cookbook** has made your cooking experience easier, healthier, and more delightful. Keep experimenting, keep savoring, and most importantly, keep enjoying the journey of creating nutritious, delicious meals—because eating well doesn't have to be complicated.

Happy air frying, and may your kitchen always be filled with the aromas of good food and great memories!

Kitchen Measurements Conversion Chart

Dry Weights

1/2 OZ	1 tbsp	1/16 C	15 g	-
1 OZ	2 tbsp	1/8 C	28 g	-
2 OZ	4 tbsp	1/4 C	57 g	-
3 OZ	6 tbsp	1/3 C	85 g	-
4 OZ	8 tbsp	1/2 C	115 g	1/4 lb
8 OZ	16 tbsp	1 C	227 g	1/2 lb
12 OZ	24 tbsp	1 1/2 C	340 g	3/4 lb
16 OZ	32 tbsp	2 C	455 g	1 lb

Egg Timer

Soft: 5 min.

Medium: 7 min.

Hard: 9 min.

Oven Temperature

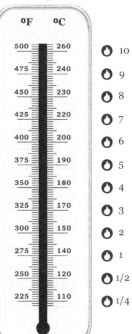

°F	°C	
500	260	10
475	240	9
450	230	8
425	220	7
400	200	6
375	190	5
350	180	4
325	170	3
300	150	2
275	140	1
250	120	1/2
225	110	1/4

Liquid Conversion

1 Gallon
4 quarts
8 pints
16 cups
128 fl oz
3.8 liters

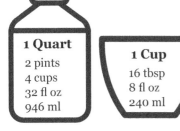

1 Quart
2 pints
4 cups
32 fl oz
946 ml

1 Cup
16 tbsp
8 fl oz
240 ml

1 Pint
2 cups
16 fl oz
470 ml

1/4 Cup
4 tbsp   2 fl oz
12 tsp   60 ml

Liquid Volumes

1 tsp = 5 ml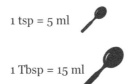

1 Tbsp = 15 ml

Dash = 1/8 tsp
Pinch = 1/16 tsp

oz	spoon	spoon	ml	C	pt	qt
1 OZ	6 tsp	2 tbsp	30 ml	1/8 C	-	-
2 OZ	12 tsp	4 tbsp	60 ml	1/4 C	-	-
2 2/3 OZ	16 tsp	5 tbsp	80 ml	1/3 C	-	-
4 OZ	24 tsp	8 tbsp	120 ml	1/2 C	-	-
5 1/3 OZ	32 tsp	11 tbsp	160 ml	2/3 C	-	-
6 OZ	36 tsp	12 tbsp	177 ml	3/4 C	-	-
8 OZ	48 tsp	16 tbsp	240 ml	1 C	1/2 pt	1/4 qt
16 OZ	96 tsp	32 tbsp	470 ml	2 C	1 pt	1/2 qt
32 OZ	192 tsp	64 tbsp	950 ml	4 C	2 pt	1 qt

Air Fryer Cooking Chart

Vegetables	Temp oF / oC	Time (Min)
Asparagus	400°F/200°C	7
Beet Chips	400°F/200°C	7
Broccoli (Florets)	400°F/200°C	10
Brussels Sprouts (1/2)	380°F/190°C	10
Corn on cob	380°F/190°C	10
Cabbage, Steaks	380°F/190°C	10-12
Carrots, Sliced	400°F/200°C	12
Cauliflower (Florets)	400°F/200°C	10-12
Eggplant, Chunks	400°F/200°C	10-12
Green Beans	400°F/200°C	7-10
Mushrooms	400°F/200°C	8-10
Onions, Chopped	400°F/200°C	10-15
Peppers, Chunks	400°F/200°C	12
Potato, Baby	400°F/200°C	15
Potato, Wedges	400°F/200°C	15
Potato Chips	400°F/200°C	8
Potato, Wedges	400°F/200°C	10
Pumpkin, Chunks	400°F/200°C	12-15
Radish Chips	380°F/190°C	8
Squash	400°F/200°C	12
Squash, Breaded	350°F/170°C	10
Sweet Potato, Fries	400°F/200°C	10
Tomato, Sliced	400°F/200°C	10
Zucchini, Sliced	400°F/200°C	10

Fish and Seafood	Temp oF / oC	Time (Min)
Calamari	400°F/200°C	5
Fish Fillet, 1 inch	400°F/200°C	10-12
Salmon Fillet	400°F/200°C	10-12
Scallops	380°F/190°C	5-7
Shrimp	380°F/190°C	6-8
Shrimp, Breaded	380°F/190°C	8

Meats	Temp oF / oC	Time (Min)
Bacon	380°F/190°C	10
Burgers	380°F/190°C	10
Chicken Whole	350°F/170°C	50-65
Chicken Breast	400°F/200°C	12
Chicken Drumsticks.	400°F/200°C	20-25
Chicken Wings	400°F/200°C	20-25
Chicken Tenders.	400°F/200°C	8
Chicken Thighs	400°F/200°C	20
Filet Mignon	400°F/200°C	8-14
Lamb Chops	400°F/200°C	8-12
Meatballs	400°F/200°C	6-8
Pork Chops	400°F/200°C	12-15
Pork Loin	380°F/190°C	12-18
Ribeye	400°F/200°C	8-12
Ribs	400°F/200°C	10-15
Sausages	400°F/200°C	12-15
Sirloin Steak	400°F/200°C	8-12

Snack/Dessert	Temp oF / oC	Time (Min)
Avocado Fries	380°F/190°C	8
Pineapple, Sliced	350°F/175°C	10-15
Mini Cheesecakes	350°F/175°C	10
Fried Oreos	380°F/190°C	6-8
Fried Pickles	380°F/190°C	8
Jalapenos, Stuffed	380°F/190°C	8-10
Chickpeas	350°F/175°C	15
Blooming Onion	380°F/190°C	10
Pizza	380°F/190°C	8-10
Toast	400°F/200°C	4
Hard Boiled Eggs	350°F/175°C	10-12
Soft Boiled Eggs	350°F/175°C	8-10

Frozen Foods	Temp oF / oC	Time (Min)
Chicken Nuggets	400°F/200°C	8-10
Cheese Sticks	400°F/200°C	7-10
Fish Filets	400°F/200°C	7-10
Frozen Fries	400°F/200°C	14-20
Pot Stickers	400°F/200°C	8-10

Two Bonus E-Books

kdpmasterinc@gmail.com

GET THIS E-BOOK FOR

FREE

YOU can get this ebook for free after sending me your name and email address.

Two Bonus E-Books

GET THIS E-BOOK FOR
FREE

YOU can get this ebook for free after sending me your name and email address.

Recipes Index

Made in United States
North Haven, CT
30 November 2024

61258966R00076